THE SLOPES
OF LEBANON

OTHER BOOKS BY AMOS OZ

AMOS OZ

THE SLOPES OF LEBANON

Translated from the Hebrew by
MAURIE GOLDBERG-BARTURA

A Helen and Kurt Wolff Book
Harcourt Brace Jovanovich, Publishers
San Diego   New York   London

MILSTEIN
DS
102.95
.0913
1989

Library of Congress Cataloging-in-Publication Data
Oz, Amos.
[Mi-mordot ha-Levanon. English]
The slopes of Lebanon/Amos Oz; translated from the Hebrew by
Maurie Goldberg-Bartura.—1st ed.
p.   cm.
Translation of : Mi-mordot ha-Levanon.
"A Helen and Kurt Wolff book."
ISBN 0-15-183090-8
1. Israel—Politics and government. 2. Lebanon—History—Israeli
intervention. 1982–   3. Jewish-Arab relations—1973–   I. Title.
DS102.95.0913   1989
956.92'044—dc19   89-2090

Design by Dalia Hartman

Printed in the United States of America

First United States edition

A B C D E

Contents

THE SLOPES
OF LEBANON

Hebrew Melodies

It was June 1987. Exactly five years had passed since the invasion of Lebanon, and everyone was trying to forget it. Radio, television, and the press held a festival to mark the twentieth anniversary of the Six-Day War. They sponsored symposia, played Hebrew songs ("I Remember Bet H'arava," "The Western Wall," "Ammunition Hill"), held memorial services at military cemeteries, expressed their nostalgia for that smashing victory, and swooned over "Jerusalem of Gold." And they also argued at length about what we describe with the loathsome phrase "the fruits of victory."

Nobody here commemorated the war in Lebanon during that week. The fallen soldiers of the Six-Day War "belong to all of us," but those who died in Lebanon belong only to their mothers now.

Until the Lebanon War, even someone like me had an admission ticket (perhaps for a place in some rear corner of the balcony, standing room only) to the enchanted world of "the beautiful Land of Israel," to the Hebrew melodies, to the feelings of "a man [who] wakes up one morn, feels he is a people reborn, and begins to move forward," in the words of A. Gilboa. During the Lebanon War, it was possible to hope that the blindness, the hunger for power, and the self-righteousness so evident then were only side effects of the war, and that when peace came, our health would be restored. But during the Lebanon War I understood, or thought I understood, at last, that the disease was deep-seated and widespread, that it might be something more than a by-product. Even now, after Lebanon, from time to time I search for something on which to pin my hope and in which to become involved. But life is not as it was before that war. What once was will never be again.

There are people on the left who, at this point, would say to me: "Good morning! Welcome to the real world." In their eyes Israel was the bad guy long before Lebanon—ever since the rise of the Likud to power,* or since the administration of Golda Meir, or since the occupation of the West Bank and Gaza in 1967, or maybe ever since the beginning of the "Zionist penetration." I do not agree with them. That debate has been aired in other places. I wrote this essay in June 1987 only in order to present what I remembered from the summer of 1982.

In August 1981, through the mediation of the American diplomat Philip Habib, a cease-fire agreement was reached between Israel and the PLO. Both sides honored that agreement along the Lebanese border. It was, I believe, the year with the fewest casualties since the establishment of our state. The PLO was distracted by its attempt to take control of wide areas in a

* Likud is the major right-wing party in Israel and led the country from 1977 to 1984.

2

disintegrating Lebanon. Another year and yet another, and part of Lebanon might perhaps have turned into a Palestinian state. And, indeed, the PLO invested great effort in establishing the infrastructure for a quasi-regular army, including several dozens of obsolete tanks and considerable artillery. Despite the exaggerations of Israeli propaganda, which publicized reports during the Lebanon War of "mammoth arms stockpiles," the organized strength of the PLO did not come close even to the strength of a single Syrian or Jordanian division. The PLO had the power to be a nuisance and to draw blood before the Lebanon War, and it continues to have that capacity after the war. But it did not have the power to pose a threat to the survival of Israel, nor can it ever, by virtue of the limits of its potential, pose unaided such a threat in the future. All was quiet on the northern front.

On the night from Wednesday, June 2, to Thursday, June 3, 1987, the Israeli ambassador to Great Britain, Shlomo Argov, was shot in the head. Abu Nidal's group claimed responsibility. The PLO spokesman in Beirut was quick to disassociate his organization from the crime, because the PLO was just then concentrating on a not entirely unsuccessful attempt to achieve international recognition so that Israel might be forced to accept it as a partner in negotiations over the future of the occupied territories. The government of Israel, however, placed full responsibility on the PLO for the attempted assassination of the ambassador. On Thursday afternoon, an acquaintance telephoned me and said, "Get ready, ol' buddy! There's going to be a little war pretty soon. Something like an expanded performance of the Litani raid in 1978. Only this time we'll go as far as the Awali River or maybe even up to the Zaharani. Find it on the map. And we won't pull back unless we can hand the whole package over to the good ol' boys of Major Haddad." And then he added another,

3

cryptic, sentence, "Unless the whole of that Lebanon falls apart completely from our kick—in which case, anything may happen."

That same night several reservists from Kibbutz Hulda were called up. Not many—maybe four or five. Early that Friday morning, convoys of military trucks, covered with tarpaulins, passed through nearby Bilu junction. At noon we could hear preparations going on at the Tel Nof air base. The regional civil-defense headquarters called our kibbutz coordinator and asked him to beef up our night watch. The army radio station began to put on special newscasts, and everything was just as it had been in the good old days, just as before the Sinai campaign of 1956, just as before the Six-Day War of 1967, just as before Yom Kippur of 1973. It was like a traveling troupe that completes its tour every few years and then returns for a repeat performance, except that in the meantime the actors have aged a bit, the old familiar stage props have become threadbare, and the whole audience recites the lines before the actors can utter the words. Only the children who have not seen the previous performances are excited.

But this time there is something missing. This time the familiar show seems to have shrunk. After a while you can feel a difference between this time and previous times; this time your stomach doesn't contract in spasms of anxiety. Also missing is the fear that the war may descend upon our own red-tiled roofs here at the kibbutz. Unlike earlier wars, no one bothers to clean out the bomb shelters or to reinforce the windowpanes with strips of masking tape, to wash the heavy blackout curtains or to make up a duty roster for the infirmary. And suddenly it dawns on you: This game is fixed. The results of this war are clear from the outset, and, in any event, not one sliver from it will reach us here. The whole war will be taking place in another country, and may Allah have mercy on them. This time our whole country is not the battlefield, nor the people the army, and this time it is not a life-and-death struggle. This time Israel will have a war deluxe, and if someone should have doubts as to whether he'll survive—well, it's only the guy who's being sent there, to the arena. The spectators can sit in the stands and munch popcorn. Or, instead of sitting and watching, they can go about their business as usual—everyone, that is, who doesn't happen to care particularly for this war. For instance, they can go abroad for that planned vacation in Spain or Portugal, or they can finally get around to enclosing that porch, or they can open that restaurant, produce that first play, or trade in that old car. I mean, of course, everyone who hasn't been called up himself, or whose loved ones haven't been drafted. This time it's not the whole nation that is at war; it is just the army, the government, and the newspapers. These lines bear witness to the abomination of this war, which was not forced upon us and was not fought to anticipate a threat to our survival, but, rather, to "achieve a result" or to "strike while the iron is hot." It's something like a timely investment in the stock market. This was never the case in Israel's previous wars, not even in those that were regarded as controversial for one reason or another. And that is the essence of the horror that Menachem Begin was to describe a few weeks later as a "war of choice," arguing that it is convenient, cheaper, and more worthwhile than "wars in which we have no alternative." And, at the same time, his followers, in order to justify this war, will try retroactively to defile the earlier wars, claiming—along with Israel's enemies— that actually we always did have a choice, that we always were the aggressor, that we always were lying when we claimed that our back was to the wall, and that Israel always flaunted spe-

cious, self-righteous arguments in order to cover up its glut-
tony; and it is no big deal, so what's the *shpiel*, and would you
kindly cut the crap and shut up.

All this surfaced only in the weeks ahead. On Friday,
June 4, there was quite a different sort of discussion around
the lunch table in Kibbutz Hulda's dining hall. M., one of
the old-timers in the kibbutz, said, "Begin is just looking for
some resounding military success to give his supporters new
inspiration and make them forget about having had to quit
our settlements in Sinai two months ago."

Redhead said, "This time we've got to finish them once
and for all, not like during the Litani operation. And if the
Egyptians make a peep, that'll be our opportunity to take back
Sinai."

Said A., "Forget about Sinai now. Reagan told Begin to
take Lebanon and give it to the Christian Phalangists. Maybe
we should keep everything up to the Litani, so we'll have
enough water for our country. And if, by chance, the result
is that Mr. Assad* falls, the Egyptians will be sending us
flowers. You can believe me. After that, maybe we'll be able
to give the Arabs a slice of the territories, or a little autonomy,
and that'll be that. We might just come out from this deal
with a comprehensive, total peace, on our own terms."

M. said, "Begin just wants to go down in history as more
of a Ben Gurion than Ben Gurion. And that Raful [Raphael
Eitan] and that Arik [Ariel Sharon]—well, they've had itchy
trigger fingers for a long time."†

L. added, "All those bickering factions in Lebanon will

* Hafez al-Assad, born in 1928, has been president of Syria
since 1971.
† Ariel Sharon, general, politician, and a leader of Likud, was
minister of defense during the Lebanon War. Rafael Etan, also a
general, was chief of staff 1978–1983.

6

come to us for help in putting their houses in order. The Christians, the Druse, the Whatzits, and even the Palestinians themselves, after the way the Phalangists and the Syrians slaughtered them at Tel Azaatar."

Redhead said, "It's all an American plot. Maybe they worked the whole thing out at Camp David, sort of on the quiet, on the side. And do you know what? Hussein and the Saudis are going to lick their lips when Arafat's end arrives. It's going to be a great little war! The Three-Day War—that's what they'll call it."

That afternoon, alone at home, I lay on the couch and read the weekend newspapers. I wondered whether I, too, was going to be called up for reserve duty. I hoped I wouldn't be, and I was a little ashamed of that hope. The afternoon papers struck a tone of forced gaiety, as though the old marching tune this time had a counterfeit ring. If you believed the papers, Israel was like an aging gentleman, portly and well established, who locks himself in the bathroom to get spruced up for a prurient rendezvous that has come his way without any effort on his part. Humming to himself before the mirror, he tries to get into the proper spirit with memories of his wild youth, when his back ached from all the pats of admiration.

But now, the code words from the days of 1967 sounded tired and worn out. "A preemptive strike," somebody wrote. "To take them off the playing field for the next ten years," another analyst explained. And someone else even resurrected the one about "reviving the element of deterrence." They wrote that our peace treaty with Egypt would prevent the opening of a second front on that side and allow us a lightning victory "in view of the balance of power," particularly if the Syrians had the good sense to sit this one out. They also wrote about the need to "root out international terrorism at its source, once and for all." Someone else, in fatherly, forgiving tones, appealed to the leaders of the opposition Labor party to remember—for their own good—that they had paid dearly in the elections of the year just past for their opposition to the bombing of the Iraqi nuclear reactor. This time, the journalist advised the Labor leaders,* they ought to go along with the people and not act against them.

That afternoon, Israeli Air Force planes launched a massive bombing attack on the suburbs of Beirut. They destroyed, as the newscasts reported, the municipal stadium, which had served as a huge arsenal for the terrorists. The flames, it was gleefully reported, "could be seen for dozens of kilometers." The evening news informed us, as usual, that "Arafat himself had miraculously escaped from the bombing."

Later that evening, at long last—as promised, as written in the program—the army radio station started to broadcast old-time Hebrew melodies: "There in the Hills of Galilee," "In the Eucalyptus Grove," and perhaps even "Mount Hermon's Majesty" ("We climbed with the wind/ to her shining peak . . .").

All day long, that Saturday, the Israeli government waited for the PLO's response to the bombings near Beirut the day before: flurries of Katyusha rockets on the villages of Galilee, which would provide justification for an invasion. For a full day and night, the PLO managed to restrain itself, perhaps because its leaders sensed what was about to happen and did not want to play into Israel's hands.

On Saturday morning, M. and I drove in the kibbutz Subaru to a meeting of Peace Now supporters in the kibbutz movement, which took place at a kibbutz in the north. All

* The Labor party, the major center/left-wing party in Israel, led the country from 1948 to 1977. Since 1984, it formed a "national unity" coalition with Likud and other parties.

the northbound roads were jammed with long military convoys: tanks piggybacked on huge carriers, mobile artillery
pieces, jeeps, trucks open and closed, some of them towing
enormous spotlights and others dragging elongated tools of war
covered by khaki tarpaulins, buses filled with soldiers (none of
whom were singing), and among the vehicles, as always in the
wars of David against Goliath, there were civilian trucks that
had been drafted: Berman's Bakery, Tadiran Co., Amcor En-
terprises, Marbek, Inc., and so forth.

At the kibbutz conference, they talked as usual about the
"corrupting occupation" and about the "nationalist-religious
fanaticism" that had shown up "in all its ugliness" two months
earlier, during the evacuation of the Jewish settlements in the
Sinai Peninsula. They condemned false messianism and
warned about the "waning of the spirit of Camp David." Opinions were aired for and against Yigal Allon's plan for territorial
compromise. A young woman with an American accent compared Israel to the United States in the Vietnam War and
expressed her understanding of the "Palestinian resistance
movement." And there was a slightly built, emotional young
man—from Latin America, I think—whose name I have forgotten, but whose words I remember well. He said that there
was going to be a blitzkrieg in Lebanon and, as a result of the
quick and easy victory, Lebanon would become West Bank
Number 2. First they'd occupy half of Lebanon to prevent
Katyusha attacks. Then they'd say there was no one to give it
back to because there was no one to talk to. Later, they would
say that perhaps there was someone to talk to, but that without
a stable and durable peace we will return nothing. Whereupon
they would say: What's the noise all about? What occupiers
are you talking about? What occupation? Why, all we did was
liberate the biblical portion of the tribe of Asher. And then a
squad of rabbis would be sent to renovate the ruins of an

ancient synagogue in Nabatiyah or a Jewish cemetery in Sidon. After that, a settler's group from Gush Emunim (Bloc of the Faithful)* will set up house there in order to pray at the grave of Queen Jezebel. And then lands will be expropriated for military maneuvers and installations. These lands will be held by paramilitary settlement groups with such names as Cedar Trees and Leaders, to prevent incursions by local fellaheen into restricted military areas. These settlements would support themselves by growing cherries for export, and when they were handed over to civilian authorities they would live on tourism and skiing in the snowy Lebanese mountains. The centrist United Kibbutz Movement would refuse, at first, to set up kibbutzim north of the generally accepted boundary, the "Katyusha range," along the Litani River. The Ha Shomer Hatzair Kibbutz Movement would agree to settle only within a "cosmetic distance" of several hundred meters from the old border. In the early years, only Gush Emunim followers would settle north of the Litani. The rabbinate would decree that the Bible forbids us to turn our ancestral inheritance over to the Gentiles, and that decision will receive wide support because this ancestral inheritance also happens to be very important for defense and very strategic as well as rich in water and arable land, which will gradually be expropriated. Apart from that, they will say that no one except ourselves has a historic right to Lebanon, which was, after all, the artificial creation of French imperialism and, when you get down to it, there is no such thing as a Lebanese people anyway: Lebanon already exists in Syria. Besides, the Arabs already have enough territory, and if they don't like it, they can lump it and go back

* Gush Emunim is a spiritual-political movement that seeks to build Jewish settlements throughout the Israeli-occupied territories, in order to retain "greater Israel," including the West Bank and Gaza. It consists mostly of religious Jews.

10

to their own countries. The upshot of all this will be that, twenty years later, the right will refuse to relinquish a single inch, while the left, taking a balanced, realistic stand, will propose a territorial compromise: annex only the territory up to the Litani and return the rest in exchange for a true, stable, and lasting peace with appropriate security arrangements. That's what will happen.

A giggle rippled through the audience at the young man's words. Many thought he was exaggerating a little.

(Four months later, a government spokesman was to make a slip of the tongue that spoke volumes, "The Israel Defense Forces will not pull out of Lebanon until the Syrian Army, too, pulls out of Syria." Under the Dostoevskian title "Crime and Punishment," Rabbi Dov Lior would soon publish an article in the *B'nai Akiva Journal* in which he would claim that the war in Lebanon was a punishment from heaven for "the sin of having handed over the Sinai Peninsula to the Egyptians," but at the same time it was the beginning of the Redemption, since we had liberated the Land of Cedars, which, according to the Bible, was part of the inheritance of the Children of Israel who had gone forth from Egypt. We had been commanded, as far back as the days of Joshua, son of Nun, he said, to conquer it, but had been a little remiss about this until now.)

Toward evening M. and I returned from the conference at Kibbutz Ma'ayan Tsvi. By twilight we had counted almost 150 tanks headed north on tank carriers. The car radio showered us with nostalgic Hebrew melodies, not the marching songs other nations play on the eve of war, but soul-melodies full of charm and longing: "The Two of Us from the Same Hometown," "Oh, the Open Road," "Night of Roses," "I Bear the Pain of Silence."

To what tribal codes did those melodies address themselves? What did the tribe want to whisper to itself in the few precious hours that were left before it set out to overrun Lebanon under a pretext that was mendacious, self-righteous? What emotions were those cloying tunes meant to arouse—or to silence? Perhaps this: That we are beautiful, gentle people, righteous, pure, and sensitive, completely out of touch with our actions; that we will be forgiven because our pure and poetic hearts know nothing about the filth that is on our hands; that the evening scent of roses will come to perfume the stench of dead bodies that will pile up by the hundreds and thousands in the days to come.

The hands are the hands of Begin and the voice is the voice of the Geveatron Kibbutz folk choir.

Since the Sabbath had come and gone without a barrage of PLO rockets on the villages in Galilee, the air force was sent on another bombing raid on Lebanon on Saturday night. It was clear that Israel would not tolerate the self-restraint of the PLO and would not countenance Arafat's decision to keep quiet. And indeed, just as the architects of this war had hoped, the barrage on Galilee came on the night between Saturday and Sunday. Most of the shells fell somewhere between the villages, not on them—this time. Only one person was wounded and almost no damage was done—in the words of the official announcement, which, this time, seemed to carry a slight undertone of frustration. The PLO spokesman, on the other side, said something about a "warning response."

That same night some more reservists were drafted from Kibbutz Hulda. Over early-morning coffee in the dining hall, the local pundits were saying that "they are going to grandstand it." H. stopped me near the laundry house. She was almost at the end of her pregnancy and she told me that her husband had been called up at dawn that morning. Then she burst into tears. I, in my great wisdom, told her in authoritative tones that everything would be just fine, that it would all be over in just a few days.

That afternoon several Israeli military formations crossed the Lebanese border along several main axes. Afterward a task force was put ashore north of Sidon in order to block enemy routes, and perhaps to cut off lines of retreat as well. During the night between June 7 and 8, Israeli forces gained control over the forty-five-kilometer area between the international border and the Sidon-Jezzin line—that same area the government spokesman had initially declared to be the goal of the "operation." Fierce fighting continued in that area for another week with PLO troops that included little boys carrying RPG bazookas, who holed up mostly in the refugee camps between Tyre and Sidon. The entire population of Sidon—men, women, and children—was ordered to leave their houses and to assemble at the seashore. Air force planes were sent, wave after wave, to bomb the firing sites in the Rashidiyeh and Ein-al-Hilwah refugee camps and Sidon itself. The trouble was that those gun emplacements happened to be in the midst of densely populated side streets, and thousands suffered death and destruction. ("Well, who told those bastards to hide behind old women and children?")

The official spokesmen used the deceitful name "Peace for Galilee" (no war, not even a justifiable war of defense, can be called "peace"). They talked a lot about "innocent women and children"—in the villages of northern Israel. (The women and children of the other side are not innocent, and, of course, men are never "innocent.") They talked about intolerable provocations (although the year prior to the war had been calm to an unprecedented degree). They talked about "enlightened world public opinion" (which very quickly became "the hypocritical world"). They talked about "limited objectives, which have been achieved almost entirely thus far" (while the Israeli forces had been given orders to engage the Syrian Army and drag it into the war). From newspeak to newspeak, the radio continually perfumed the airwaves with "The Scent of the Apple, the Blush of the Rose," "The Forgotten Melody Returns," "Let It Be, Let It Be, All That We May Ask, Let It Be," "Would That All Lovers," and a new song: "Do Not Uproot the Sapling." Behind the deceitful screen of folk melodies and self-righteousness, the decision was made to broaden the scope of the war. The Israeli formation, which had reached the Shouf Mountains and was met by the local population with applause and a shower of rice, was now ordered to advance to the Beirut-Damascus highway and there to link up with our Christian brethren, who, anticipating their liberation, were busy preparing royal banquets for us. The decision was apparently made on June 8, if not much earlier—if, indeed, it had not been part of the original plot of calculated disinformation. That same day, the Syrian forces were overrun at Jezzin; Syria finally got the message and entered the war.

It was a war of deceit and brainwashing, the true goals of which had been concealed from the nation, from the soldiers, from the Knesset, and from most of the Cabinet. Under the guise of peace for Galilee, Begin was going to crown the corrupt Gemayel family as rulers over all Lebanon, and turn Lebanon into a client state of Israel. ("So what? Why is it okay for Brezhnev? Why is it okay for Assad?") He was going to strike at the Syrian Army although it had not provoked Israel and had not caused a single Israeli casualty during the eight years since the signing of the Syrian-Israeli agreement at the end of the Yom Kippur War. He would do the Western world ("the ingrates!") a favor by finishing off the PLO and thus, as these geniuses saw it, putting an end to the Palestinian problem. He would win, as Chief of Staff Lieutenant General Eitan put it, "the war for the Land of Israel" (in other words, for the territories that we occupied during the Six-Day War), and perhaps clean up, once and for all, the mess in the Middle East. The history writers were asked to take note that, unlike the Christian world, which had stood aside while Jews were being slaughtered, the Jews had not stood aside, but had gone to the rescue of their Christian brethren in Lebanon (to save them from the disaster they had brought down on themselves). The role of the sweet, innocent Little Red Riding Hood was thus given to the rotten Christian Phalangists, whose creation had been inspired by fascism. Begin assumed the role of the noble woodsman who rescues Little Red Riding Hood from the jaws of the Islamic wolf, if not the role of the last Crusader.

Indeed, if we are to judge by his speeches during that war, Menachem Begin went into Lebanon to fight a worldwide war against the enemies of Israel, from Amalek to Chmielnicki to Hitler: an awesome retribution for all that the Jews had suffered. Once and for all.

"We love you, precious Homeland/ in joy, in song, and toil/ Down from the slopes of Lebanon to the shores of the Dead Sea/ We will rake your fields with plows. . . ." On June 9, the Israeli Air Force swept away virtually all the ground-to-air missiles the Syrians had installed in the Lebanon rift (without asking our permission!). In air battles that same day, twenty-nine Syrian planes were shot down, with all Israeli planes returning safely to their base. The following day, the Syrian forces were struck near Lake Karoun and the Syrian First Division was defeated in heavy armored fighting. During the night between June 10 and 11, an Israeli spearhead force reached the Beirut-Damascus highway. The Lebanese capital was cut off. (I am told that the code name for Beirut in Israel Defense Forces documents was "Bar-Lev," which is not only

15

the name of Haim Bar-Lev, the Israeli Army's deputy chief of staff during the Six-Day War, but the Hebrew acronym for Birat Levanon—the capital of Lebanon.) Fifteen thousand Syrian soldiers and PLO fighters were trapped in what Arafat would later glorify as "the Palestinian Stalingrad."

Y. came over to see me later that evening. "You see?" he said. "We screwed them quick, hard, and neat." "This won't end well," I said. I didn't know what else I could have told him. "Are you starting that all over again?" said Y. "You'd do better if you got up the courage to send an article to *Davar*, that newspaper of yours, retracting all those gloom-and-doom prophecies you've been publishing these last few days. You're making a fool of yourself."

Then came the cease-fire of June 11, which wasn't a cease-fire. And after that came the battles of Aley and Bachamdoun and Baabdeh and the Galerie Semaine Square, spiced with parties and fancy banquets given by the Christian Phalangists (as their contribution toward their own liberation) honoring officers of the Israel Defense Forces and delegations of Israeli dignitaries. Then came two months of cruel siege of the city of Beirut, including massive shelling of residential neighborhoods, which cut off electricity and water. Meanwhile, in Israel, the rift deepened between those who supported the war and the critics who publicly demonstrated their protest. There was controversy even among the soldiers, many of whom discovered they had fallen victim to a cynical lie—that they were being used to achieve objectives of which no one could have conceived at the beginning of the "operation." High-ranking army commanders aired criticism of the plan to enter West Beirut. Colonel Eli Geva was relieved of his command and dismissed from the army because of his refusal to take part, as commander, in an operation he considered unconscionable. Public opinion in Western nations was not ecstatic about the Israeli crusade "to rescue the Christians in Lebanon." Strong criticism of the military operation quickly escalated into poisonous criticism of Israel and of Zionism itself, with more and more blatantly anti-Semitic undertones.

On August 21, in accordance with an agreement reached under American auspices, the beleaguered Syrian and PLO forces were evacuated from West Beirut. A multinational force was supposed to take their place in the city. Two days later Bashir Gemayel was elected president of Lebanon by the vote of a phony parliament ringed by Israeli tanks. Within three weeks Gemayel was murdered by Syrian agents, and the Israel Defense Forces quickly took control of West Beirut. In coordination with the Israel Defense Forces, the heroic Phalangists, who until then had not lifted a finger to help "save the Christians," took upon themselves the task of "purifying" the Palestinian refugee camps in the city. Within earshot of Israeli army positions, the illustrious Phalangist heroes of Eli Houbeike and his cohorts, their way lighted by flares of the Israeli Army, slaughtered men, women, and children in the Shatilla and Sabra camps.* "The Phalangists went overboard this time," said Chief of Staff Eitan without elaborating. Speech is silver. . . .

Then from all the radio stations, simultaneously—as though by command from the top—the charming Hebrew melodies suddenly vanished. The Israeli nightingale seemed to have swallowed its tongue. Other songbirds were heard in

* In the Shatilla and Sabra refugee camps on the southern outskirts of Beirut, eight hundred Palestinian civilians were murdered by Lebanese Phalangist forces in 1982. In the worldwide uproar that followed, Israel was blamed for allowing the Phalangists to enter the camps.

the land, including the grenade explosion that murdered Emil Grunzweig, the Peace Now demonstrator, and wounded some of his friends in the square in front of Begin's office.

And then began the retreat from Lebanon and in its wake came amnesia. Uncle Sharon was forced to leave, Uncle Raful, the chief of staff, went away, and Grandpa Begin was gathered up into his own bosom. The entire Lebanon War was retired to the cellars of collective oblivion. Some seven hundred soldiers were gone, along with thousands of the enemy. And gone, too, it is said, were more than ten thousand civilians, "innocent" even in the vocabulary of those who had abetted the crime.

And in time we started playing those melodies again— "How Shall I Bless," "He Will Bring Us," and "Would That Buds Could Speak."

It is time to go back to the beginning—the beginning of that war. To a picture of Menachem Begin, pale, leaning on a cane, surrounded by his generals and his advisers, at the top of captured Beaufort, the old Crusader castle in southern Lebanon. The blood of the dead from the previous night's battle has not yet dried beneath his feet, but this man is standing there, "tired but happy." Happy? Gleeful and arrogant, crowing that this "great" fortress had been captured "with no losses." And with fatherly satisfaction, he questions one of the stunned soldiers: "What used to be over here? Machine guns?" Then, as though assuming the role of a Biblical king in a Cecil B. De Mille spectacular, he "bestows" Beaufort upon the armies of Major Haddad.

Thus began the new era: King Solomon granted "forty cities" as a gift to Hiram, king of Tyre; Israel dispensed fiefdoms to its vassals.

18

This was only the prologue. Several days later, the prime minister appeared on television, bemused, sarcastic, in a verbal blast against all the Gentile hypocrites ("Look who dares preach morality to us!"). He trampled upon his domestic opponents, promoted Arafat to the rank of a new Hitler, and in the next breath demoted him to the rank of a "hairy-faced" two-legged beast, treating viewers at home to a "strategic" comparison in which he contrasted "Hannibal who had outflanked the Romans one way," with his own minions, "who had, on the contrary, outflanked both this way and that." What his words did not reveal was written on his face: He was smug. To listen to him, the war seemed like a toy that had finally been presented to him after a long, frustrating wait, which had gone on, perhaps, since his youth. Pugnacious, petty, and vengeful toward his opponents, and indifferent to the horrors of the war, he was consumed by a hatred of "the Gentile world," born of a feeling of inferiority that was cloaked in a pose of sarcastic superiority. "And now," he happily promised us, "there will be peace in the land for forty years."

As fate would have it, several months later Begin himself became a "hairy-faced" man. Photographers were requested to show tact and to refrain from photographing him with the stubble of mourning he had grown in accordance with religious custom after the death of his wife and, later, not with the beard he grew because he was stricken by a skin disease. Some say he was stricken by remorse as well.

But what do I care about Begin? May he find a little peace in his seclusion. We will cast no stone on his sufferings. The guilt for Lebanon lies not with Begin alone, and certainly not just with Eitan and Sharon, who carried out his orders (or carried out his orders and then some). We will have to grit our teeth and admit that this war was a war of the people. The people wanted it and the people (most of them) supported it, took pleasure in it, and hated the handful who were opposed. At least that is how it was until the war got "bogged down"; at that point, this good people simply forgot about the war and its dead.

But who are "the people" in this case? We cannot simply place the spilled blood at the doorstep of the ecstatic masses who shouted "Begin! Begin!" Many of them celebrated the war and spat their hatred in every direction, but they weren't the ones who had started it and they weren't the ones who allowed it to go on. The Labor party and the centrist Shinui party (Democratic Party for Change), and some of the members of the dovish left wing of the Knesset, either voted with the government or abstained in the vote of no confidence when the war broke out. M. K. Imri Ron, of the left-wing Mapam, was photographed in his army uniform and his officer's insignia, calling upon his party to support the war and not to incense the people. Labor's Motta Gur volunteered to serve as Sharon's unofficial adviser. And Labor party leader Yitzhak Rabin recommended "tightening the siege on Beirut." Thus spoke the representatives of enlightened Israel, the land of the pioneer folk songs. And even *Ma'ariv*, the afternoon newspaper, published a political cartoon, portraying the Israeli army, tiny but unyielding, standing all alone against a ferocious, hairy terrorist giant, armed to the teeth, while a knife held by Peace Now is being plunged in the back of the brave little IDF.

In Tel Aviv and the development towns, at kibbutzim, just as in Juniyeh, the Christian suburb of Beirut, the dead died and the bathers bathed in the sea, businessmen transacted business and vacationers took package trips to Scandinavia— returning, of course, in time for the opening of school for their children. No one heard, or could have heard, the wail of an air-raid siren. No one (except the Israeli residents along the northern border during the first two nights) hurried into bomb shelters. The newspapers were filled with Lebanese cherries, with obituaries, Beirut restaurant reviews, nightclub features in the Christian enclave, and shouts of merrymaking. There were endless television broadcasts of joyous Lebanese civilians showering the rice of welcome on Israeli military convoys and just a handful of left-wing pictures of burning cities, maimed children, and weeping women. ("They're used to that sort of thing over there," several newspapers wrote. "Why, up there in Lebanon, slaughter is a way of life.")

And the radio dipped it all in the oil of idyllic nostalgia while Begin and his friends presented the ongoing horror as a sort of neurotic mixture of a new Eichmann trial (with Arafat, if and when he was caught, in the lead role), the Sinai campaign in an expanded edition (with Israel in the role of scourge for the Western world), together with the fall of Nazi Berlin (with Arafat's bunker cast as the bunker of Adolf Hitler), and "The Six-Day War Rides Again" (down to the "poetic" touch of identical dates), topped off by "healing the trauma of the Yom Kippur War" (in the words of the Great Traumatizer).

Right up until the BBC reported the slaughter that the Phalangists had conducted by the light of our flares in Shatilla and Sabra. Until Emil Grunzweig was murdered by a hand grenade intended for all the opponents of this war. That grenade closed a circle: Jerusalem had gone off to clean up Beirut and now Beirut had reached the heart of Jerusalem to turn Jerusalem into a Beirut.

Not one popular song was born out of the Lebanon War; except "Planes come down from up anon/ Taking us to Lebanon/ For Sharon, O, we will fight/ And come home in coffins tight," which was composed by defeatist soldiers, plunging their knives into their own backs. Perhaps it would have been proper to set to music the poems of despair, anger, and loss written during those days by Israel's poets, young and old, or the elegies written by Raya Harnik for her son Goni, the Peace Now activist, who had died at Beaufort, and then to play them on the Hebrew hit parades. But no, the metabolism of the idyllic Hebrew melodies would not have been able to absorb them. So they would have no place even among such elegies to heroes of past wars as "A Palmachnik Named Dudu," "In the Plains of the Negev a Defender Fell," "Accept, Ye Hill of Ephraim, This New Young Sacrifice."

There would be no more songs about "The Bitter and the Sweet," only about the bitter and the hasty.

Seven years have passed since then. I have tried to replace my alienation of those days with various kinds of involvement, engagements, petitions, and public stands. This collection of essays deals with these issues.

There are times when I forget a little, when I try to persuade myself that the "people" learned a lesson, that they have learned—the hard way—the limits of power, that there's a catch in a philosophy based on violence. There are times when I think that "it" can't happen again.

Perhaps.

But among the victims of the Lebanon War was "the Land of Israel, small and brave, determined and righteous." It died in Lebanon perhaps precisely because, in Lebanon, its back was not to the wall. *It* was the wall and *they*, the Palestinians in Lebanon, had their backs pressed to the wall. From underneath the "ponytail and pinafore" of the myths, the claws peeked out. Just as they continue to peek out daily: not only in the occupied territories, but also in the "good Israel of old"—in the suburbs and in the cities, on the crazy peripheries as well as in the enlightened, sane center, in the slums and on the campuses, among the hotheads and among the intelligentsia, and in the heart of the corridors of power.

After Lebanon, we can no longer ignore the monster, even when it is dormant, or half asleep, or when it peers out from behind the lunatic fringe. After Lebanon, we must not pretend that the monster dwells only in the offices of Meir Kahane; or only on General Sharon's ranch, or only in Raful's carpentry shop, or only in the Jewish settlements in the West Bank. It dwells, drowsing, virtually everywhere, even in the folk-singing guts of our common myths. Even in our soul-melodies. We did not leave it behind in Lebanon, with the Hezbollah.* It is here, among us, a part of us, like a shadow, in Hebron, in Gaza, in the slums and in the suburbs; in the kibbutzim and in my Lake Kinneret—"O Lake Kinneret mine, were you real or only a dream? . . ."

That which you have done—whether it be only once in your life, in one moment of stupidity or in an outburst of anger—that which you were capable of doing—even if you have forgotten, or have chosen to forget, how and why you did it—that which you have done and regretted bitterly, you may never do again. But you are capable of doing it. You may do it. It is curled up inside you.

This book includes several articles I wrote in recent years. They are arranged in parts, by subject matter, and more or less in chronological order. Most of the essays were originally

---

* Hezbollah is a militant, armed Shiite group in Lebanon, sponsored by Iran.

printed in *Davar*; some appeared in *Yediot Aharonot*. The first part deals with my reactions to the Lebanon War, during and after. Much of what I saw then was included in my book *In the Land of Israel* (1983), and therefore, understandably, does not appear again here. But I would like to emphasize the ineluctable connection, in my eyes, between *In the Land of Israel* and this book.

WHAT ARE THEY
DYING FOR?

Hitler's Dead,
Mr. Prime Minister

*"If Adolf Hitler were hiding out in a building along with twenty
innocent civilians, wouldn't you bomb the building?"*
        —Menachem Begin, in answer to his critics

No, sir. Your parable is invalid, and the very idea of such a
comparison shows a serious emotional distortion. Issar Harel,
the former chief of Mossad, and his men captured Adolf Eichmann without harming even his immediate family. Perhaps
it would have been better if you had asked Harel, the day after
the criminal shooting of Ambassador Argov in London, just
how they did it, instead of listening to the brutal advice of
General Sharon and General Eitan.

The words that follow are addressed to you, Mr. Begin,
not to your advisers. Adolf Hitler destroyed one-third of the
Jewish people, among them your own parents and relatives,
and some of my family. There are times when, like many
Jews, I feel sorry I didn't kill Hitler with my own hands. I'm
sure you feel the same way. There is not, and there never will
be, any healing for the open wound. Tens of thousands of
dead Arabs will not heal that wound.

But, Mr. Begin, Adolf Hitler died thirty-seven years ago.
Pity or not, the fact is: Hitler is not hiding in Nabatiyah, in
Sidon, or in Beirut. He is dead and burned to ashes.

27

Time and again, Mr. Begin, you publicly betray a weird urge to resurrect Hitler from the dead just so that you may kill him over and over again each day: sometimes cast as Chancellor Helmut Schmidt, at other times in the role of terrorists, or the Soviets, or Bruno Kreisky, or the Iraqis, or virtually every Gentile who has ever fought us or opposed our conduct. This urge to revive Hitler, only to kill him again and again, is the result of pain that poets can permit themselves to use, but not statesmen. For them, it's dangerous. You, Mr. Begin, are not—at least not to the best of my knowledge—a poet. Some of your feelings have been expressed in blood and fire, not in rhymed couplets. Even at great emotional cost personally, you must remind yourself, and the public that elected you its leader, that Hitler is dead and burned to ashes.

You also must remind yourself that now, at the cost of the blood and sweat of four generations, the people of Israel have a state whose existence is at present under a double threat: not only from an enemy that seeks its extinction, but also from our own well-known tendency to extreme hysteria tinged with messianic madness; a tendency that has brought catastrophe and destruction upon us before in our long history.

As for the PLO, I once had my hopes and illusions, but I have abandoned them. The PLO is indeed unwilling, and apparently unable, to make any concession acknowledging the very existence of Israel. And that is why the PLO is continuing the brutal, wretched tradition of the fanatical Palestinian leadership that brought down one calamity after another upon its people. To this extent we can be in agreement, you and I. To this extent I would support, in principle, your position with regard to fighting the PLO (although not the simplistic, clumsy, sterile battle you are launching now in Lebanon). But you didn't lead us into this particular war in order to destroy the PLO. You led us astray.

Your real purpose is to reduce the Palestinians to a submissive group of serfs brought to its knees within the Greater Israel of your fantasies. This goal of yours is neither humane, nor realistic, nor in keeping with Jewish tradition at its best; nor is it appropriate to mainstream Zionism, which agreed, time and again, over decades, to partition this land between its peoples (on the bases of various lines)—until you turned up and reneged on this consensus.

Your withdrawal from the historic Zionist position of compromise with the Palestinians was encouraged, of course, by the stubborn refusal of the Palestinians to make any compromise at all. But this withdrawal contains the seeds of a disaster that threatens our very existence no less than do our enemies. If you deny the identity of one nation, you will eventually come to resemble those who deny your identity.

I am addressing you, not your followers, some of whom openly advocate doing unto our enemies what our enemies are striving to do unto us. I have no basis for argument, nor even a common language, with them. If we want to turn Israel into a copy of Russia, the oppressor of national entities, or of Assad's Syria, or of the PLO and Iraq, what good does it do us to spill our own blood in a war against those we are trying to copy? Better to assimilate with them, to be barbarians of the Mosaic persuasion, and to draw the curtain on the Zionist dream of creating a just and enlightened society here. You, Mr. Begin, have declared more than once (far from the populous town squares of Lod and Netanya) your devotion to humanist ideals. So it is to you that I turn and ask: Why did you lie to the people? Why, in a massive bombing attack on Beirut, did you deliberately and cold-bloodedly provoke the enemy and drag him into a barrage in Galilee? Was it in order to have an alibi for invading Lebanon and to create a "new order" there? Why did you choose this year, which perhaps had the fewest casualties since the establishment of the State of Israel, to initiate a calculated war? Why did you send the Israel Defense Forces (you never call the IDF by its name— you always refer to it as "our army" or "the army of Israel"; this is not by accident!), for the first time since we achieved independence, to fight, not for our survival, not to repel an attack, not to save Israel, but in order to obtain "advantages" and "gains"? (Advantages and gains for whom? Only time will tell.) This is the first time we have gone to the battlefield as though to the stock market: a correct investment (perhaps), a cautious gamble (as it were, "striking while the iron is hot," "reasonable" risks and "relative" sacrifices). There has been nothing like it since the beginning of modern Zionism. Until now we have gone out to kill and be killed only when our very existence was at stake. I am talking about the threat of extinction, not about infiltrational harassment.

The goal of this war is not "peace for Galilee." You have misled the nation; just like those whom you and I have always despised, you have given the name "peace" to a calculated, instigated war. The purpose of your war is to break the back of the Palestinian people, to install a "friendly" regime in Lebanon and to create—at the cost of the lives of soldiers— conditions to make your dream of a Greater Israel come true. But even so, if you were to stand up in the midst of the fighting, if you were to stand up tomorrow or the day after, and propose to the Palestinian people once again the historic compromise that has characterized the mainstream of Zionism, then, per- haps, the blood will not have been spilled in vain.

Mr. Prime Minister, there can be either a compromise, albeit a painful one, between the two peoples in this land, or else perpetual war. There is no third alternative.

The entire nation, or most of it, wanted peace for Galilee and peace for the whole country and hoped for the emergence of a Palestinian leadership with whom we could talk. But you took advantage of this consensus, and of the self-sacrificing spirit of our soldiers, for purposes that are acceptable only to your own party and its fellow travelers, and perhaps not even to all of those. You summoned the soldiers to battle in the name of that broad consensus, but you abused that consensus for the sake of goals that are rejected by at least half of this nation: "Greater Israel," the destruction of a Palestinian identity, "the entrapment of Hitler," changing the regime in Lebanon, and prospects of political dividends.

I do not question, Mr. Begin, your legal right to use your majority (of sorts) in the Knesset to involve us in a war that you desire. We have not disobeyed, nor will we disobey, your orders to report for duty. The parliamentary majority (some of it acting as though bewitched) is in your hands, and we are left to grit our teeth. But your lie will not be forgiven: You called upon our soldiers to sacrifice their lives for goals agreed upon (though the manner in which agreement was arrived at is subject to debate), but in fact you led them to kill and to die for goals to which a great many of us are opposed. Please do not come to comfort our mourners: You have caused a rift unlike any that has ever been before. Half the nation is turning its back on you in resentment, in fury, and in grief. But then, I think that this final sentence should really be addressed to the leaders of the opposition, not to you.

Yediot Aharonot, June 21, 1982

Where Can We
Hide Our Shame?

Grandiose exercises in geostrategy have always been the favorite pastime of the Revisionists, our hawkish right wing. As early as sixty or seventy years ago, Vladimir Ze'ev Jabotinsky would move armies with a breath from his mouth, draw new frontiers for many nations, set superpowers against one another, and reorder the world with a flourish of his sharp pen, as though straining to supply the Zionist enterprise with a crown of invisibility or with seven-league boots.* Sometimes the Labor movement would react to these whims with a faint smile, like a wise old man watching a child.

Menachem Begin, who does not have Jabotinsky's poetic talents, did inherit from his mentor the lust for drama and for

---

* Jabotinsky (1880–1940), Zionist leader, novelist, poet, thinker. Born in Russia, he was one of the founders of Jewish self-defense groups during the Tsarist pogroms of 1903–4; was an officer in the Jewish battalion of the British army in World War I; led the national-liberal faction of Zionism, 1925–1940. Jabotinsky was inspired by nineteenth-century European romantic nationalism.

the euphoria that comes from sweeping, impetuous moves. Although circumstances made it virtually impossible for Jabotinsky to go beyond writing articles and composing poetry, Begin woke up one morning with an accelerator and with a real steering wheel in his hands: all the power of Israel, power that had been built, piece by piece, step by step, sacrifice by sacrifice, by four generations of Zionist pioneers.

And Begin used that power in the name of peace for Galilee, for purposes very remote from peace and very far away from Galilee.

This is the first of all our wars in which we went to battle not to repulse a threat to our very existence but to get rid of an irritant, and mostly to change the map of the region.

One can argue about the most effective course of action against the terror of the PLO: Is it best to use the full strength and power of the IDF, or is there, perhaps, another way?

> *Wherever our foe turns*
> *We will shadow him day and night;*
> *Into his inmost chambers,*
> *Pursuing his every footstep,*
> *Armed with a sleeping draught,*
> *And with a slender needle.*
> —NATAN ALTERMAN

Above and beyond the argument about what methods of warfare to use, there is the simple fact that a dispute between the two peoples who live in this land cannot be solved by force. If we do not seek a solution through compromise, the bloodletting will never end.

But the Begin government did not initiate this war for the sake of establishing peace for Galilee. Peace for Galilee has gradually become—or was it actually meant to be, from the outset?—an excuse for the realization of a typical Jabotinskyan fantasy: to cut the knot of historic conflict between us and the Palestinians with one smashing blow; to change the face of Lebanon and perhaps even that of Syria; to help the Americans contain the influence of the Soviet Union; in short, to create a dramatic turning point in the whole scenario. This intention was disguised so that the Labor party leaders could be dragged, as though possessed, into giving a weak and stammering "Aye," seemingly agreeing with Begin on the essentials, even as they tugged at his sleeve, begging him to slow down, just a little.

This business will not end well because this time, once again, the leadership of the Labor party has failed to understand the tear that Begin is making in the fabric of our national consensus of many decades—a consensus by which we launched a full-scale war only when our very existence was in danger, a consensus by which we responded to irritants and attrition only with limited, measured, calculated use of military force, only with "a slender needle."

I don't want to speculate or express all my apprehensions here. The fighting is still going on, and each day the dead are being gathered up from the battlefield to be brought home. Could it be that Begin and his government are planning yet another round of war—"peace for Lebanon"? "peace for Syria"? "peace for the Free World"?

If the Labor movement continues to stand paralyzed by fear of the masses and continues to be satisfied with mealy-mouthed, whining mutterings about how "we were not party to the preliminary consultations," then there may be no point to its continued existence. It might be better if it climbed onto Begin's bandwagon, or perhaps even joined the Likud ("as an autonomous faction!") and tried, as the current saying goes, "to change Begin from within." Its place will then be taken, of necessity, by a different opposition, which will declare courageously: There is an abyss between us and the hawkish right wing. We seek an honorable compromise, while they fantasize about a decision made in blood and fire.

In the meantime, until we have an opposition here, where will we hide our shame?

Davar, June 22, 1982

On Wonders and Miracles

The war was born of a lie. From the very start, it was a war initiated by Israel, a ready-made war waiting only for an opportunity or an excuse. It wasn't intended to fend off a threat to Israel's very survival. It was intended to rid us of a relentless irritant, even though that irritant in fact hadn't been felt for the last ten months. There had been complete quiet along the Lebanese border. Not a single casualty in ten months in the towns and villages of northern Israel. It is spurious to claim that the war began on Sunday, June 6, 1982. It began on Friday, June 4, 1982, at three o'clock in the afternoon, with a massive air raid on PLO targets in Beirut; the intention was to provoke the PLO into shelling villages in Galilee. But this was already a rerun of a previous performance. There had been an earlier attempt, in April, "to provoke a shelling barrage on Galilee"; however, at that time the PLO refused to play ball. But this time their stupidity won out, and they did start a barrage.

"Peace for Galilee" is a deceptive phrase. War, even when it is fully justified, should not be called "peace." Only in the world of brainwashing and tyranny described by George Orwell do such slogans as "War is peace," "Slavery is freedom," and "Ignorance is power" prevail.

Begin's true goal was the classic Jabotinskyan one: to use force not in order to repel force, but primarily to reshuffle the world, to install a pliable regime in Lebanon, to conduct a "preventive" war against Syria, to wipe out the Palestinian problem, to perform a free service for what Begin likes to call "the free world." In short, to change the face of the Middle East in one blow. Begin knew very well that there was no national consensus on these goals, so he chose a spurious starting point from which to deceive not only the soldiers, not only the opposition, but even part of his own coalition.

I do not understand the tendency of many mainstream Labor party people these days to assign the responsibility for this war to Ariel Sharon and Rafael Eitan, and to depict Begin as being led, without a mind of his own, by these two. On the contrary: Sharon is a clumsy but obedient instrument. The adversary is Begin and Beginism.

The Limits of Obedience

Begin has the legal right to give orders to the army by virtue of his majority in the Knesset, even though his majority is slim and was achieved partly by manipulation. We must remember, however, that for the past ten years Gush Emunim and its allies have used such arguments as "the will of God" and "the call of conscience" in order to trample on the authority of the Knesset—that is, the authority of the people. For ten years most of us have tried to uphold the law, rightly claiming that if this is not a people ruled by the due process of law, there will be a deluge of anarchy, civil war, and, ultimately, dictatorship. As long as this country is a country ruled by due process of law, and as long as it operates within the broad limits of international law, we must recognize this government—distasteful though it may be to some, including me—as our legal government. Here, of course, we are confronted by the crucial question: Where are the limits of obedience? A former student of mine, now an army officer, came to me and asked at what point I thought it was his duty to refuse to obey orders. Should he fight in Lebanon even though it was against his conscience? I answered: "If you refuse to obey a legal order, then anything goes. You should do this only if you have come to the conclusion that the entire state has become a criminal state." "But what if I am given an order to cut off Beirut's electricity?" he asked. I replied: "That is a legal order." "But what if I am ordered to cut off the water supply? Or to shoot at unarmed people?" he wanted to know. "In that case," I said, "disobey, and stand trial. Because that last would be a blatantly illegal order, according to the precedent set by the Supreme Court in the Kafr Kassem trial.* That would be passing the limit of obedience."

I am referring to the legal, not the moral, aspects of this war. In moral terms, this war has been unjustified from its very inception. There can be no atonement for what we did in Beirut. Even if we accept Begin's claim that an entire city has been taken over by murderers, who are holding it hostage and shooting at us from behind the backs of innocent civilians, we could not accept his conclusion that it is permissible to kill the hostages together with the kidnappers, to bomb a plane full of innocent passengers, as it were, in order to kill its

* In 1956, during the Sinai campaign, 47 Arab citizens in the village of Kafr Kassem were shot by Israeli troops. The Israeli Supreme Court convicted the soldiers and their commanding officers, and ruled that a soldier was required by law to disobey a "clearly illegal order."

hijackers. If, God forbid, the PLO were to take over Haifa instead of Beirut, would Begin give orders to bomb and shell Haifa almost indiscriminately until its terrorist captors surrendered?

But as long as the orders are legal—as long as the orders are to strike, with clear intent, only at the enemy and to try not to injure civilians—they must be obeyed. Anyone who suggests that a soldier should, in every instance, act not only in accordance with the law, but also outside the law, in accordance with his own personal moral values, is essentially suggesting that we also legitimize the conduct of the radical right. Indeed, he is suggesting that we should begin to dismantle this society and this state. And there are situations in which one would have to go that far—for instance, if your country has been taken over by a gang of criminals. But we have not yet reached that point, and I hope we never will.

The Secret of Begin's Strength

During a debate in the Knesset, when the dovish opposition raised some stammered criticisms, most of them in halfhearted, embarrassed mutterings, about the moral aspects of the war in Lebanon, Begin got to his feet and did what the nationalist right always does when it is attacked on moral grounds: It claims that the critics are hypocritical and self-righteous, because they, too, in their turn, have done unspeakable things to the Arabs. In this manner, the right retroactively besmirches all of Zionist history as one continuous crime. Thus Begin produced one foolish, obtuse interview, which Motta Gur, a Labor party leader, gave several years ago, and from which he quoted extensively and declared with provocative glee, "Look who's talking about morality! Why, Israel always did contemptible things! Israel, under a

Labor government, always bombed centers of Arab population. Israel was always what it is now!"

This argument, "Look who's talking," is a very effective weapon against both the opposition and what Begin calls alternately the "hypocritical world" and the "free world." Begin has struck a deeply sensitive chord in the Jewish psyche. In essence, he is winking at the persecuted and is offering them, in exchange for the "popular-priced" ticket of a war against Arafat, the "deluxe" spectacle of a worldwide war against Jew-haters through the ages. Hitler, according to Begin's implied message, has risen from the dead and is sitting in a bunker in Beirut. Whoever wants to kill Hitler no longer has to swallow his frustration. Hitler now "rides again," this time within reach, in a guest appearance right around the corner, and we can give him his just desserts at last. At the same time, we can give Sennacherib, Titus, Antiochus, Chmielnicki, Bevin, and Stalin, too, what's coming to them. All for a package price.

There is one more message: Our sufferings have granted us immunity papers, as it were, a moral carte blanche. After what all those dirty goyim have done to us, none of them is entitled to preach morality to us. We, on the other hand, have carte blanche, because we were victims and have suffered so much. Once a victim, always a victim, and victimhood entitles its owners to a moral exemption. (There is no difference between this argument and the claim of Palestinian leaders when they justify blanket terror: "The Palestinian people have lost everything. Therefore, anything and everything is permissible to them.")

This is a powerful, effective message. Opposition leaders have not managed to find an emotional and intellectual reply that the public will comprehend. Begin presents the war in Lebanon as an act of "settling accounts" with Jew-haters through the ages. And thus a large part of the public perceives the war in Lebanon as a "worldwide struggle" (and a neurotic one) against all our past and present foes.

This, and more: How morbid—and how effective—is the attitude that presents Israel as a ferocious Goliath ("We are the fourth superpower in the world; we have enormous power; we drove out the British; we did the Arabs in; we struck at Russia; and now we are saving the free world from the jaws of terror and from the clutches of its own weakness; and we're destroying Hitler once again"), and at the same time portrays Israel as a lamb surrounded by a pack of wolves ("We are wretched, isolated, besieged, and beleaguered; the whole world is against us; no one understands us and no one sympathizes with us"). This message gives its consumers the best of two worlds, the intoxication of power along with the pleasures of self-pity; to be both Samson the Mighty and Rachel mourning her children. Two for the price of one.

In the Knesset Committee for Security and Foreign Affairs, Begin sneered at his opponents, "If Adolf Hitler were hiding in a building along with twenty innocent civilians, wouldn't you bomb the building, gentlemen?" It is characteristic that Begin spoke of twenty "civilians," not twenty "Jews." This is the sort of autism whose most prominent symptom is the use of the expression "Jewish blood." There is no such thing as "Jewish blood." Neither in the Bible nor in the Talmud will you find even a single use of the phrase "Jewish blood." On the other hand, there is an abundance of references to "innocent blood" or "the blood of innocents." Members of the opposition don't react to this. Not one of them had the courage to say, "No, sir! We would *not* have blown up that house. We would have found a way to get at the murderer without spilling innocent blood."

Within the framework of the Beginist effort to save Leb-

41

anon, how many Lebanese, who are not the enemy, is it permissible to kill in order to "save" Lebanon from the clutches of the PLO? A thousand? Ten thousand? A hundred thousand?

Chips at the Casino

Begin himself doesn't use pretenses. The juxtaposition of the arrogance of power with self-pity, of "the God of vengeance" with "the Divine Presence in mourning," expresses his own most fundamental experiences, and, it would seem, those of most of the people of Israel. Golda Meir expressed similar sentiments in a similar world view. In her eyes, too, we were always pictured as a lamb at the mercy of vile predators. But then, she truly felt pain at the deaths of those who fell, whereas Begin appears downright gleeful and vivacious these days. Ever since the war began, his public appearances have been marked by venomous, vengeful arrogance, by pugnacious jubilation. A feeling of profound relief shows on his face and echoes no less in his voice than in his words. He looks, on the TV screen, as if he is having the time of his life and loving every minute of it.

Not long ago, he spoke at the College of National Defense. He took issue with a Zionist consensus, which had crystallized over the course of decades, that you go to war only as a last resort. In unavoidable wars, he argued, when you fight with your back to the wall, there are always heavy casualties. In wars of choice, the "price" is lower. It was as though he were talking about some sidewalk slot machine: You keep on dropping into the slot the price—the lives of children, albeit children of eighteen—and at the bottom out come assets, advantages, and gains.

From this view, the war in Lebanon is a good "cost-effective" investment. Oh, there may be investments that are even better. We could, for example, parachute several Israeli divisions onto the Iranian oil fields and annex Iran's Persian Gulf coast. Khomeini is, after all, no less an enemy than Arafat. He, too, has vowed to march on Jerusalem and finish us off. Surely the Russians will not come to Khomeini's rescue; surely the Americans will give us a pretty thank-you; surely the Iraqis will send us bouquets of flowers. All we have to do is drop in a few hundred soldiers and "win" the oil fields. All this could be done in a war of choice that may be much more "profitable" than all our previous wars put together. But when you go to war as if you were going to the stock market, when you relate to the lives of the fighters as you would to poker chips, the end of the road is a field strewn with the boots of soldiers who have run back home because they don't want to be someone else's poker chips. This is the ineluctable logic that many other nations learned after they ceased to consider war only as a last resort and started thinking of war in terms of investments and dividends.

> *Davar Hashavua*, August 20, 1982,
> based on Part 1 of an interview
> with Niva Lanir

Facing the Nation

This government must go immediately. The horror of Beirut must be investigated immediately.

Is there a contradiction between these two demands? Is this perhaps a premature verdict of guilt?

The answer is no, on both counts.

Who is "guilty" of the mass murder at the refugee camps in Beirut? The guilty parties, the murderers, are our protégés, our pets, our allies—the Christian Phalangists. They and they alone.

Who is "responsible"? The responsible party is the Begin government, and the Begin government alone. One who invites the Boston strangler to spend two nights in an orphanage cannot claim, when he sees a pile of dead bodies the next morning, that he had asked the man only to wash the ears and necks of the orphans.

What, then, must a judicial commission investigate?

It must investigate who gave the orders, and when, how, and why.

When was the administration first informed of the massacre? What did it do, or fail to do, when it found out? When did it report or fail to report it? Who lied to the nation, to the Knesset, and perhaps even to the government of Israel?

"Our hands did not spill this blood and our eyes did not see," said former Chief Rabbi Shlomo Goren on the eve of Yom Kippur, rolling his eyes heavenward.

"Your hands are covered with blood," said the prophet Isaiah.

"For they had eyes but they did not see," said the prophet Jeremiah.

Veteran defeatists, both of them. Troublers of Israel. Self-hating Jews.

May this year and its evils end together, and may wickedness be dispersed like smoke.

> *Davar,* September 28, 1982,
> written on the eve of
> Yom Kippur 5743

What Next?

These are tough times. Never before has Israel been assaulted by an almost daily bombardment of plans for agreements, suggested solutions, peace proposals: the Venice document, the Fahd plan, the Reagan plan, the Fez plan, the Hussein proposal, the Khawatme declaration, the Syrian statement. And who knows what tomorrow will bring? From good to bad, or, to be precise, from almost good to propaganda gimmicks?

The Begin government reacts to all of them as though to an evil barrage of Katyushas: sounding the sirens, urging the nation to go down to the bomb shelters, crying "foul"—and aiming a salvo of verbal fire at the enemy's position.

Actually, it is no surprise that a government that has chosen to call a premeditated war by the name Peace should react to peace initiatives as though they were declarations of war. No wonder it responds with heavy-handed indictments of animosity and ridicule; all of it, from Reagan to Khawatme, is furiously rejected out of hand.

Yet the entire range of recent proposals, some, indeed, "proposals" in quotes, and some, indeed, "peace" in quotes,

46

deserves a careful and considered response, not a high-pitched cry of panic.

Certainly there is no reason for us to give an unqualified yea to President Reagan or to say amen to King Fahd. There is no reason for us to fall on the necks of the Syrian gentlemen or of Naif Khawatme. But neither is there any need to barricade ourselves on the rooftops, sniveling and crying that it's all lies and deceit, shrieking that we reject it all, out of hand, that it must never materialize, that we will never agree or let ourselves be seduced—never, not ever, not for the rest of eternity. That is the style of this regime. And the style of this regime is very sick.

A normal nation, like a normal person, when enemies approach with peace proposals, wisely invites them in for a cup of coffee. If they accept, fine. We will sit down with them on the front porch and bargain, soberly, patiently, and reasonably. If they don't accept, then their insincerity will be exposed for all to see, their bluff called, and we will be blameless.

"One doesn't ask a man where he spends his nights," Begin spouted haughtily. So be it. The nocturnal adventures of the prime minister are an issue between him and Mrs. Begin, and we will maintain a tactful silence. But, by all the rules of etiquette, we are entitled to ask this man and his friends what they do during the daylight hours, hours during which statesmen—at least between one revilement and the next—get paid to sit and negotiate with friends and sometimes even with enemies. Why don't they invite all these peacemongers for a cup of coffee and a session of political give-and-take? Does Reagan have some new ideas for the resolution of the Middle East conflict? Welcome, Mr. President, have a seat; would you like a brandy or perhaps some coffee or a cold drink and some cake? And then we'll tell him politely that paragraph three seems quite nice but, by your leave, we have a different suggestion in place of paragraph five. Are King Fahd, King Hussein, Foreign Minister Khaddam, or that esteemed terrorist Khawatme offering us a peace plan that is deceitful and dangerous? Won't you come in, Your Majesties? The first door on the right. It's good to have you here at last, Mr. Syria. By the way, dear Mr. Terrorist, we are in the habit of leaving our submachine guns in the cloakroom. Please be seated, gentlemen. We'll be very glad to listen to what you have to say, but after that, will you kindly listen to what we have to say? And if we can't settle the issue today, maybe we'll be able to settle it after three or four more meetings, or another ten or twenty. Your opening proposal is unacceptable to us. So sorry. Would you be kind enough to try again? We, too, will think hard and try again. It was so good of you to come. We'd be delighted to return your visit. And in the meantime, let's all stop shooting and go on seeing each other.

That is the way a sane human being responds to a peace proposal. That is the response of a sane nation.

And what do we do?

For us, the style is the government, and the style of this government is insane. Here, for example, are two recent pearls of wisdom:

"Only Arik Sharon can prevent various and sundry meddlers from stealing southern Lebanon from us, after the Americans managed to snatch Beirut from us . . . under the pressure of public hysteria unleashed by the Labor party" (from a public statement of the Liberal party think tank). What intellectual honey! What liberalistic incense! Why, their own mothers wouldn't be able to recognize them, these latter-day Liberal thief-catchers and traitor-hunters.

"After this war . . . our enemies will learn to be careful and not even sneeze anywhere near Israel" (Knesset member

Yigael Horowitz in a public interview). Bless you, Mr. Horowitz. Warm regards from all the arrogant and haughty phrases that were buried—together with three thousand of our boys—after Yom Kippur 1973.

Indeed, not another sneeze or cough, not a yawn or a hiccup on the turf of this Beginist Israel. No more peace initiatives and no more proposals for solutions. Not even a little bird will be allowed to chirp around here. Please don't say "Shalom" when you meet Israel in the street; she may go berserk with fury. Please don't knock on the door. Please don't call us on the phone. And do not sneeze in our vicinity: We are sick here.

And what next?

We will overcome. This, too, shall pass. And we will recover.

Davar, June 6, 1982

A Siege within a Siege

IN MEMORIAM EMIL GRUNZWEIG

(Remarks made at a Peace Now rally, Jerusalem, February 17, 1983, at the end of the seventh day of mourning after his murder)

One week ago, on this spot, our friend Emil Grunzweig was murdered. We still do not know who murdered him and tried also to murder many of his friends. But we know that Emil died because of his love of freedom, of peace, of justice, of Israel, and of life itself.

Life and peace, justice and freedom, like Israel itself, are under siege. This siege has been neither broken nor eased as a result of the brutal war in Lebanon. On the contrary, the siege is becoming increasingly acute and intense, a siege within a siege. Emil lived, fought, and died within a circle of hatred and violence. And he paid with his life for his attempt to break that awful circle.

The Zionist undertaking and the State of Israel were born out of a wonderful dream and a great hope perhaps unparalleled in all history: to return to the land of our forebears, to build it and to be built by it in peace, and to create in that land a just, enlightened society, a society that would free the creative energies hidden within us, spreading light to our neighbors and to the entire world.

Three generations of brutal Arab siege and fifteen years of the corrupting occupation of the Arab zones have served to entrench within us emotions of fear: fear of the Arabs, fear of the outside world, and fear of peace itself.

This fear has gradually turned into fury and hysteria, directed, ironically, against those of us who strive to free the people from the circle of hatred and fear, against those who fought on the battlefields, in the intensity of war, and returned from there to struggle for peace.

Emil fought on the battlefield against Israel's enemies, but he fell by the hand of other enemies: enemies of freedom, enemies of law and justice, enemies of peace.

We do not yet know whose hands spilled his blood. But we know that whoever murdered Emil tried to murder an idea and a faith. And we know that the deed only strengthened the idea and deepened the devotion, even as it shocked the overwhelming majority in this nation.

We know, too, that slogans such as "There's Only One Way" (the slogan of Meir Kahane and the extreme Right) and "Only by Force" may yet destroy what no enemy from the outside will ever succeed in destroying: the spirit of Israel, its inner strength, its image as a brave, enlightened, free nation.

What else has to happen to us, for God's sake, before we will come to our senses? What else must happen to this nation before it will understand that it is a sin, a crime, a folly to pin everything on the question: Where will our borders be drawn? What else has to happen to this nation before all of us will realize that a nation can blow itself to pieces from within, even inside expanded, enlarged borders? What else has to happen before we will understand that, in this ambitious frenzy to expand our boundaries, we have already gone almost beyond all bounds? What else has to happen before we will discover that a nation can unite and recover from the plague of violence and hatred only through peace, not by extending its authority over a foreign people by force of arms?

About ten days ago the Committee of Judicial Inquiry publicized its findings with respect to the massacre at Sabra and Shatilla. And we saw, as though illuminated by a flash of lightning, two souls scrabbling inside the body of Israel: one humane, the heir of the moral tradition of the prophets and of the Jewish-Zionist vision of justice; and the other, which I will not describe here this evening. Whatever the future of the present government may be, I believe that the report of this commission will continue to shine like a beacon in the dark night around us. Because this report is a document that spells out the very heart of the controversy: Shall justice pierce the wall or shall justice be broken by a hand grenade?

The crime that was committed here one week ago today did not mean tragedy for just one family, one group, or the Peace Now movement; it was a shocking tragedy for the entire nation. This time, many people, some of them ideologically remote from us, expressed their shock. Let us silence, for a moment, the accumulated bitterness and doubt that, perhaps, nips at our hearts, and let us try, with all our might, to believe that everyone who expressed grief and shock was indeed shocked. Let all of us, whatever our views may be, make a supreme effort to conduct a penetrating national debate without letting that debate breed hatred.

We wish, from this spot, to make three appeals: one to the Palestinian enemy, one to our Israeli adversaries on the hawkish right, and one to those of our own people who share our views.

First, a few words to the Palestinian people. For decades, the path of terror and violence, that path of extremism and destruction, has brought you one tragedy after another. Your

hatred has bred only hatred. Your extremism has created coun-
terextremism in our midst. And we have all paid the price in
blood more than enough, both you and we. Our friend Emil
fought you on the battlefield and, after returning home, struggled to his last breath for reconciliation with you. As we stand
in the place where his blood was spilled, we call upon you,
the Palestinians, to take, with no further delay, the path of
reconciliation and compromise. To our own call for "Peace
Now," respond, without delay, with the same two words,
"Peace Now."

Next, a sentence or two to those Israelis whose views differ
from our own, people who—hopefully—value the integrity of
the Greater Land of Israel, and one or two other integrities as
well. We call upon you to reconsider your way, to ask your-
selves whether it is right and fitting and even worthwhile, for
the sake of your aim of territorial expansion, to tear the nation
to shreds? What has this alien fire you have kindled brought
down upon us all? To what depths may the path you have
chosen yet lead us all? What will you have gained from a
Greater Land of Israel if the soul of the nation has been torn
in two, when the abyss yawning between you and us threatens
to swallow all that was built here by the blood and sweat of
four generations?

Finally, a few words to ourselves, all those gathered here
and all those who are not here but whose hearts are with us.
Many years ago our forebears used to sing "We came to the
Land, to build it and to be built by it ourselves." They strove
to realize all their hopes here, in the lovely land of our fathers.
They hoped to live "a life of purity, a life of freedom" here.
We will never abandon that dream. We will never be tempted
to answer hatred with hatred, no matter whence that hatred
might come. Our problem is not how to protest more loudly,
or how to defeat our adversaries, or how to repay that for which

there can be no repayment. Our problem was and remains how to gain more public support, how to draw people closer to us, how to convince them of the justice of our way. And none of this can be done in a storm of fury or by clamorous shouts, but only by remaining true, persistently and courageously, to the voice of reason, moderation, and wisdom.

I appeal to all those assembled here, and to all kindred spirits, not to be caught up by hatred, not to fall into despair. We must continue the struggle for which our friend and comrade Emil gave his life: the struggle for Israel's soul.

The poet John Donne wrote, "No man is an island . . . every man is a piece of the continent . . . therefore never send to know for whom the bell tolls; it tolls for thee." As for the grenade that was thrown here, at this spot one week ago, let us never ask at whom it was aimed. It was aimed at each and every one of us.

What Are We Dying For?

According to one version of history, this year—1982—is the one hundredth anniversary of the modern-day return to Zion. What began approximately one hundred years ago at Petah Tikva (The Gate of Hope), Rishon Letziyon (First in Zion), and other places with names of similar symbolism has now reached the small mountain towns of Bachamdoun, Aley, the Presidential Palace, and the Galerie Semaine Square in Beirut. What began with the biblical words "Zion shall be redeemed by the law" has come to "Nobody's any better than we are, so they should all shut up." What began as a revolutionary decision by a handful of Jews to reenter history and operate within it has now come to be an increasingly widespread desire to transcend history in an ecstasy of messianism. What began as an aspiration to be a "light unto the nations" and continued as an attempt to be a "nation like all others" has now come to be a whining demand that "the world" permit us what is permitted to Assad and Arafat.

It is a widely held misconception that the incursion into Lebanon was a case of a compulsive gambler's not knowing

when to leave the gaming table. Even inside the Labor movement there are voices wailing in these tones: "If only they'd
stopped after the first forty kilometers! If only they hadn't entered West Beirut! If only they hadn't tried to be kingmakers
in Lebanon!" In short, if only this war had been conducted
by a Labor government instead of a Likud government, everything would have turned out just fine." But the tragedy of the
war in Lebanon is not due to a faulty sense of proportion. It
is the result of the perverted use of power. A straight line,
frighteningly consistent, leads directly from the ideological
principle formulated by P. M. Begin in his lecture to the
Academy of National Security—the principle of wars of
choice, or wars for profit and gain, which are, as it were,
"cheaper" than wars fought with our backs to the wall—to the
result: the massive killing we carried out in Lebanon even
before Sabra and Shatilla and to the unholy alliance we sealed
with the murderers of children against other murderers of
children. And it leads to deep dissension within our nation,
to unrest in the army, and to our failure, in Lebanon.

Some of our soldiers tell us that, especially during the
Lebanon War, even more than in previous wars, they were
strict about the moral aspects of their task. Pilots tell of returning more than once to their base with their bomb bays
still full because they weren't completely sure about the positive
identification of their targets. Perhaps there really was an attempt to preserve the standards.

However, the standards themselves, the standards of the
war in Lebanon, were completely new. A building of seven
or ten or fifteen floors in Beirut razed, together with its
hundreds of occupants, by aerial pin-point bombing or by a
carefully aimed artillery barrage, because our troops had been
fired upon from one of its windows. Had the Israeli Army

fought by such a standard in the Six-Day War, hardly a single building would have been left standing in East Jerusalem.

Almost unnoticed, the standards were changed. The moral code of the battlefield changed. The definition of what is forbidden and what is permissible changed. It all began with the excuse that was used to justify the war: a terrorist bullet shot into the head of the Israeli ambassador, Shlomo Argov, in London. If our criterion for going to war was, as in the Lebanon War, response to terrorist action, we would not have been involved in five wars, but in five hundred, or more. This was not just a new variation on the theme of the national consensus; it was, quite simply, a revolution. Begin and his associates knew exactly what they were doing in recent months when they began their intensive effort to rewrite history, when they tried to conjure up the ghosts of the Israeli bombing of Irbid (1970), the destruction of the Egyptian Suez-Canal cities in the battle of attrition (1969–70), even the Christian and Syrian massacre of the Palestinians at Tel Zaatar (1976), in order to justify their own doings in Lebanon, declaring that this was no place for self-righteousness—after all, Israel has always been murderous and savage. This is exactly the way in which they justify the confiscations of Arab land in the West Bank, claiming (with hysterical distortion) that, after all, Tel Aviv and all the kibbutzim, too, were built upon land that once belonged to Arabs. The crux of the claim is simple, primitive, and therefore effective and even compelling: We were always bullies, we have always dispossessed others, we always committed murder to take possession of land, and so all those bleeding hearts should kindly stop playing holier-than-thou, because their hands are no less covered with blood.

Yes, Israelis have committed war crimes in the past. But no attempt was ever made to make those crimes the norm.

There was never this whining self-righteousness, which maintains that, because they were victims in the past, the Jews are morally entitled to turn others into victims today.

The Israeli War of Independence, at least until the invasion by regular Arab armies on May 15, 1948, was, indeed, a total war, not between armies, but between two entire populations—neighborhood against neighborhood, village against village, street against street, house against house. In a war of that kind there are civilian casualties and populations are uprooted. Perhaps that is why the hawks among us look back with such nostalgia upon the War of Independence and its horrors: Just let there be another total war of life and death— just one more, please—and the Arabs will hightail it out of here, and Greater Israel will live happily ever after.

But we must remember that the wars which followed the War of Independence of 1948 were never total wars of one whole population against another, but wars of one army against another. During the Six-Day War, in 1967, the Arab inhabitants of Gaza, the West Bank, and other places waved white flags, almost without firing a single bullet at their conquerors. The realities are not the same today. Now, in the case of Lebanon, a deceitful effort is being made to depict this war as a total war in order to justify the new standards and norms of morality. As though the populations of Sidon and Tyre and Beirut were posing a daily threat to the lives of the residents of Haifa and Tel Aviv, as was the case in 1948, and therefore "it's them or us," and presumably, what we have done in Lebanon becomes permissible.

Consensus

This brainwashing is on no account to be taken as part of the argument about how we should conduct an all-out war against the PLO, which is waging an all-out war against us. But is there a chance of winning an all-out war if you don't offer your enemy, together with the battle, an honorable peace proposal, which, sooner or later, he may choose to investigate instead of fighting to the bitter end, feeling that his back is to the wall? This also touches on the specious question of "our right to the land." (The question is specious because, in the context of historical reality, rights are not a matter between man and God, but between man and his fellow man, his neighbor, his enemy. A right that is recognized by no one but yourself is not a right; at best, it is a claim or a demand.) It also touches upon a question that is not specious: Where can, and where should, our borders be drawn? Essentially, this question of standards, of what is forbidden and what permitted, of the limits of the legitimate use of force, touches upon the roots of our national consensus. Having used this term, I would like to say a few words about the lost honor of the term "national consensus"—a loss that can be counted as one of the lamented victims of the Yom Kippur War of 1973.

I say a victim of that war because, in their anger, people confused "consensus" and "conformism," and after that Yom Kippur they threw the distinction straight into the trash can. But a consensus, unlike conformity, does not mean that an entire people must think the same thing or till the same furrow, and that every deviation is foolish or perverse. A consensus is an agreement between partners, who accept certain basic rules so that they can work together. Without a minimal consensus there can be no nation-state, not even a newsstand with two partners.

There was a consensus, not complete but quite far-reaching, on the critical question "What are we dying for?" There was agreement that the return to Zion is worth paying for with human lives if there is no alternative. This applied also to the

59

independence of the State of Israel. There was virtually no pacifist Zionism. A pacifist nation is almost inconceivable. We were not asking the Arabs for permission to build our homeland, nor have we been dependent on their advice or consent. But you go to full-scale war only when your very survival is at stake. When there is attrition, harassment, or terror, you sometimes react with a selective military response, but you go to war only in times of real danger to your very existence. To be sure, this consensus has been put to the test by various "opportunities" and on various "occasions"—that is, whenever our neighbors were in some confusion and we stood to gain something from it. Some savages and bloodthirsty peoples may sometimes have considered us ridiculous because of our past self-restraint. More than once we have held back where another nation would have struck, and we have struck only selective, partial blows where some other nations would have rushed into an all-out war. We launched full-scale wars only when our enemies arose to smite us—not when they merely harassed us, not when someone declared that he wanted us dead, and not when someone stated that he wanted to wipe us out someday in the future.

We may have had to pay a price for this self-restraint, but it brought us some important advantages in terms of wide foreign support and of alliance with various segments of the Jewish people outside Israel. Above all else, this self-restraint was a crucial component of our power. Power is, after all, built not only by the primitive multiplication of a given number of tanks and airplanes by a given number of square kilometers; but also, first and foremost, upon the willingness of people to go to battle for it, upon the readiness of fighting men to lay down their lives for it. Until Lebanon, there were almost no instances of Israeli soldiers asking themselves or their comrades, "What are we doing here on this battlefield anyway, and why were we sent here?" With all the doubts, the distress, and the hesitations expressed in *The Seventh Day: Soldiers Talk* (published after the Six-Day War), you will not find a single expression of doubt about the decision to go to war in June 1967. Even during the Sinai campaign of 1956, about which I have some doubts in retrospect, there were persuasive reasons to fear that within several months Gamal Abdel Nasser would have been strong enough to achieve his openly declared aim of destroying us. My friend General Israel Tal has made a distinction between *preemptive* war, in which the enemy has created preconditions for war and is preempted by us only in a technical sense, and *preventive* war, one fought to prevent a potential threat that may or may not come to pass. He sees preemptive war as just and moral, but preventive war as morally problematic. The war in Lebanon, seen in terms of this distinction, was not preemptive and not even preventive, but a war initiated with no intention of thwarting any threat, immediate or potential, to our survival. In 1956, by contrast, Nasser was preparing to defeat and destroy Israel, and he was not far from attaining the concentration of strength he would have needed to achieve his goal.

This was not true in the case of the war in Lebanon. The Syrian Army was far from attaining total superiority over the Israel Defense Forces, and although the PLO certainly constituted a threat in the sense of a nuisance, it could not be considered a destructive threat.

A national consensus functions like any piece of material: If you stretch it sufficiently, it becomes thin and weak. If you continue to stretch it, it will tear and develop holes. History is full of examples of governments that sent their armies to war for some gain, not in order to repel a threat to their national survival. Their soldiers were by no means thrilled at the prospect of dying for the sake of one kind of profit or another. By this I do not mean soldiers writing "sob stories"; I mean soldiers who throw away their boots and go home, because the battle seems pointless to them, and because, even if they fail to fight in that particular war, their lives, their freedom, or the lives of their loved ones will not be in any danger. I do not want to spread alarm; we have not reached that point yet, and, let us hope, we will never reach it, but the line that Menachem Begin presented in his lecture at the Academy of National Security logically leads to such a point. If it is a war of choice, then let only volunteers fight it. Even a war that may break out in the future over the Greater Land of Israel (rather than over Israel's survival) would then have the internal logic of a war fought by a volunteer army. To whoever cannot live without a Greater Land of Israel, go ahead, I say, and volunteer to defend our presence in Nablus and Ramallah. The tragedy is, of course, that if a war fought over Nablus and Ramallah is lost because of an overextension of the national consensus, it will not end in Nablus and Ramallah. The hawks should give this some thought: It is better to draw the red line around national objectives that are less pretentious and more generally accepted. The more grandiose the goals, the less ready will people be to sacrifice their lives for them. As this willingness decreases, so does the strength itself. And when our strength atrophies, not only do we lose the grandiose goals, but also our more modest aspirations are endangered. (This is an additional distinction I learned from General Tal.)

Some people delude themselves, saying that the ones who broke the consensus during the invasion of Lebanon were dubious characters: left-wing journalists and writers, effete "Peace Now-niks," and treasonous self-haters influenced, perhaps, by American and European leftists from the Vietnam War, working to undermine a "heroic consensus."

Nonsense! The consensus, together with the trust, was

broken from within, not from the outside; from among the ranks. You cannot send men to battle if they are not convinced that the battle is necessary. In previous wars, there was no need to convince them. In this war there is no way to convince them. If the fighting men do not participate of their own free will, it is doubtful whether they will be fighters at all—for a while, perhaps, by force of habit, by virtue of the past consensus, but not for long.

Labor's Failure

As long as the war in Lebanon looked good and had popular appeal, most of the leaders of the Labor movement stood cheek by jowl with Begin and carried his toolbox for him. At most, there was a slight undertone of envy of Begin's unhesitating use of the tools the Labor movement had been accustomed to consider its own creation, its own monopoly. At a later stage, the Laborites hinted that they "had not been consulted in the policy-making process" (as though a government has a formal obligation to ask permission from the opposition before it decides). Afterward, they started to see the "mess" and suggested to Begin that he ease up a little on the accelerator. Only after the murder of Bashir Gemayel, which shattered the "dream of Lebanon as a vassal of Israel," and the slaughter in the refugee camps at Sabra and Shatilla, and only after the mass demonstrations organized by Peace Now had made it clear to the Labor party's leaders that there was unprecedented widespread opposition to the war from their own constituencies, did they remember to venture that this war wasn't to their liking. And now, in response to the Reagan peace plan (later rejected by all parties), they are trotting out, once again, the Allon plan. It is sad to see how the latter, which represented an interesting and creative approach in its day, has undergone a process of ritualization, having been transformed from a political proposal to a dogmatic article of faith. (For the dovish left, there has been a parallel ritualization, of the idea of an independent Palestinian state alongside Israel. This, too, has been transformed from a political proposal resulting from the pressures of reality into an exclusive article of faith.)

The Obsession with Borders

It is not only the Allon plan and the idea of a Palestinian state alongside Israel that have become dogmatic articles of faith, not unlike the tenet of "the Greater Land of Israel." The question of the final borders of the State of Israel has become, for almost all of us, on all sides of the controversy, a mono-mania. Instead of the difficult but fruitful arguments about the purpose of the Zionist undertaking and its master plan, the meaning of Judaism in our day, the attainment of a just society, the formation of a cultural identity, civil rights, the rule of law—instead of these, preeminence has been taken by the wearisome, arid question of where the borders of the state should be drawn. It has been raised for the last fifteen years as the major item, if not the only item, on our agenda. All the other issues, including those concerning Judaism in our day, have become subordinate to the border issue. One would think that countries with extended borders are, by definition, wonderful, just, secure, and prosperous, and that countries with "unsatisfactory" borders have no chance of survival. With all due respect to the Jordan rift and those eastern mountain ranges, to the Golan Heights and the Gaza Strip, what is worrisome is what is within these borders, what the character of this country and its society will be. Will it attract Jews from other lands or will it repel them? It is not difficult to imagine a country falling apart within broad, easily defensible borders,

64

or a country within narrow borders whose socioeconomic position is strong, whose citizens are full of enthusiasm, and which is able to defend itself well, precisely because its citizens are at peace with the fabric of their existence.

The border monomania is a partial explanation for the gradual, continuous weakening of the Labor movement. Here, perhaps, are the seeds of its spiritual downfall, which led, in turn, to its political downfall. In the argument about where the borders will be drawn, Begin and Gush Emunim have a message that is simple, appealing, and easy to understand, whereas the Labor movement's position is more complex, hypothetical, and more difficult to present. In the short run, at least, without the influence of a painful dose of reality, a simplistic message has a natural advantage over one that is more complex. Nonetheless, in other areas—social, economic, cultural, spiritual—and with regard to human rights and the individual's place in society, the Labor movement had a persuasive message for many people. Labor has compromised that advantage since 1967, when it was tempted into taking the political battle into an arena most convenient for the nationalist right wing: the question of borders. This has led not only to political deterioration, but also to intellectual impoverishment, to endless, dreary quarrels in favor of the Jordan rift but against Samaria, in favor of the Golan Heights but against the mountains of Hebron—a meaningless, shallow, dead-end argument for all sides.

We ought to turn to basics once again.

> Based on comments made in a discussion
> among kibbutz members at
> Yad Tabenkin Research Center,
> October 28, 1982

Of Slaughter and Distinction

The terrorist plot to blow up Arab passenger buses and to murder, in cold blood, dozens or even hundreds of men, women, and children confirms the dreadful suspicion that has haunted the public at least since the attempted assassination of West Bank mayors and the murder at the Islamic College in Hebron: Yes, there is a Jewish terrorist organization.

The aim of this plot was not to satisfy an urge for vengeance, but to set off a chain reaction: an ever-spreading bloodbath that would lead to total war, which, in turn, would lead, with the help of God, to the mass expulsion of the Arab population, which in turn, with the help of God, would put an end to the threat to peace for the next hundred years. And so the Redeemer will come to Zion.

The suspected plot was thwarted, thanks to the fine work of the Israeli secret service. Perhaps some of us should apologize—at least in our hearts—for the doubts and suspicions we harbored about the diligence and professionalism of the secret service in this case.

But now, it would seem, this emotional whirlpool of fury,

fear, and relief has begun to suck Israel's moderates into a storm of passions. We should beware of the temptation to execute vengeance on our political and ideological adversaries. We had better beware of doing to them, "on this happy occasion," what some of them have done, and are still doing, to us on every occasion: launch an indiscriminate moral pogrom.

Stated in simple terms, I am convinced that the path of Gush Emunim will lead to nothing less than national disaster. I am also convinced that the Jewish terrorist organization was leading us to the brink of impending national disaster. But we must, under no circumstances, juxtapose these two certainties. Under no circumstances should we label every Jewish settler in the West Bank a terrorist and a murderer.

I would like to believe the Gush Emunim leaders, who immediately condemned both the intended massacre and crimes that had already been committed. This does not, however, exempt them from badly needed soul-searching and, possibly, urgent housecleaning.

None of us is freed from the moral obligation to draw a firm dividing line between bad and worse.

Gush Emunim is evil not because it is a terrorist organization, but because its path will lead to one bloody war after another and to a grave distortion of Israel's character. The Jewish terrorists are evil not because they are religiously observant, not because they have hawkish views, but because they have committed crimes and attempted to commit a mass slaughter of innocent people. I believe that if we do not make an effort to distinguish between various degrees of evil, we ourselves are ultimately bound to become the servants of evil.

NOTE: It is important to point out here that, as a longtime opponent of "environmental punishment" (the practice of blowing up the homes of Jewish insurgents, begun by the British during the period of the Mandate, and adopted by the Israelis in dealing with Arab rebels), I hereby urge the military authorities not to blow up or to seal up the homes of suspects, and especially not to deport to the opposite bank of the river Jordan, without trial, the spiritual instigators of terrorist crimes.

Davar, April 30, 1984

The Power and the Purpose

What divides Israel, within itself, today?

Some say the issue at the heart of the controversy is the question of desirable and feasible borders. Others contend that Israel today faces a rebellion of Sephardim—primarily those from North Africa—against the hegemony of Ashkenazim, whose roots are in Eastern Europe. Still others point to the widening gap between religious and secular Jews as the focus of the internal struggle. Some note a contradiction between a welfare-state ideology, on the one hand, and an acquisitive, egotistic mentality, or between an increasing loss of human feelings and a growing nationalist emotionalism.

All of these divisions do exist. Israel is not split down the middle on two sides of one single divide. It is split up by lines that intersect one another at various points.

Foreign journalists, for their own convenience, sometimes tend to simplify the picture and to arrange it along a single barricade. It is easier to report to their readers on a Jewish West Bank settler who "devours Arabs" and who is, at the same time, a deprived Sephardi and a religious zealot, or,

by way of contradistinction, on an educated, secular Ashkenazi
Jew who favors compromise with the Arabs and the protection
of individual rights. To their dismay and to our good fortune,
the reality is not that simple. The vast majority of the Jewish
settlers in the West Bank are Ashkenazim, not Sephardim.
The most extreme religious zealots do not live in the West
Bank and are not the spearheads of hawkish positions. Most
Sephardi Jews do not observe the Jewish religious laws. The
left is not composed only of workers, and the right is more
populist than capitalist.

A Federation of Visions

From the beginnings of modern Zionism, some one hundred
years ago, it was a tense federation of varying, even contradictory visions, pursuing a continuous struggle, sometimes
overt, sometimes repressed, over differing basic programs,
which, despite all the conflicts, found a way of maintaining
a fragile operative balance. Here, as in every society, we note
a ceaseless tension between integral and differential forces. In
fact, the differential within Zionism tends to be more vocif-
erous; the integral is sometimes latent. At several junctures in
Zionist history—during the 1930s, and again during the Begin
years—there were warning signs of an impending explosion,
and dire prophecies were heard about an "unavoidable civil
war," which had been avoided thus far because the hidden
integral was ultimately stronger than the exposed differential,
because the anger was released only in angry words, and because of the unifying effect of threat from the outside. Perhaps
the most important achievement with which we can credit
Shimon Peres, during his two years as prime minister, from
1984 to 1986, is not the decline in the level of inflation but
the decline in the level of internal animosities and in the

emotional octaves of some of the domestic debates. This is true even though the anger and the fury, just like the differences over inflation and the territories, are still in the "occupied" stage, neither resolved nor liberated.

The civil conflict that has been going on in Israel for decades is, for the most part, a war of words, in which each side gives ulcers and heart attacks to the other. We would do well to remember that some civilized nations evolved their present identity from bloody civil wars. England was molded by religious wars, America defeated America in a civil war, and France beheaded France with guillotines, not to mention the history of the Germans, the Italians, and the Russians. Here in Israel, on the other hand, during one hundred years of Zionist solitude, despite all the painful internal conflicts, no more than fifty Jews, from DeHaan down to Grunzweig, have been killed by other Jews over differences of belief or opinion. This was so perhaps because the reality here is indeed one of a mosaic rather than one of opposing sides of a barricade. There is no overlap between the social cross section and the religious cross section, nor is there overlap between these two categories and a cross section of countries of origin, nor between these three and a cross section of hawk versus dove, and so on. On the benches of the Moscow-oriented Israeli Communist party in the Knesset you will find a middle-aged Ashkenazi from Lithuania and a young Moroccan. Four or five nonreligious parties in the Knesset have representatives who are Orthodox. Four or five parties are represented by millionaires along with residents of slum neighborhoods. Three or four parties have a hawkish wing and a dovish wing. Almost every faction in the Knesset includes Askenazim and Sephardim. Countries of origin have hardly any significance in the spectrum of opinions: David Ben Gurion and Menachem Begin, Shimon Peres and Yitzhak Shamir all came from Poland.

71

Chaim Weizmann and Vladimir Zeev Jabotinsky came from Russia. David Levy, Moshe Shahal, Shoshana Arbeli, and Moshe Katzar all came to Israel from Arab lands. Golda Meir, Moshe Arens, Abba Eban, and Meir Kahane spent their formative years in English-speaking countries. Former generals Yigal Allon, Ariel Sharon, and Yitzhak Rabin were all born in Israel. One can find Orthodox representatives (including rabbis) of both the extreme right and the extreme left among the hawks and among the doves.

The early pioneers used to sing, with passion, "Here in the lovely land of our forefathers all our hopes will be fulfilled." But from the beginning these hopes were varied and even contradictory. Some sought "to restore our days as of old," to re-create the kingdoms of David and Solomon. Others came to the land with a burning faith in "the beginning of redemption," believing they heard the stirrings of the Messiah, or intending to hasten his coming by mystical methods. There were prophets and those who sought to stone prophets. Some sought to create a Marxist paradise to which "Russia itself will come and bow down." Others had no desire to establish an independent state, but dreamed of covering the land with a network of intimate Tolstoyan communes in which individuals would attain religious revelation and wondrous purification by renewing their bonds with the forces of nature and by working the land. Some envisioned a blending into the Semitic-Arab landscape, a return of the Jews into the bosom of the family of Oriental peoples. And there were those who, like Theodor Herzl, yearned to create a Middle Eastern replica of Emperor Franz Josef's comfortable, bourgeois Central Europe, with good manners, red-tiled roofs, gemütlichkeit, and absolute quiet between the hours of two and four in the afternoon. Others brought with them, translated straight out of the Polish, a militaristic, nationalistic sentiment, a romanticism based on cavalry charges, martial yearnings, visions of blood and fire, and lofty deeds of bravery. Others saw Zionism as the only way of creating a Jewish-Hebrew cultural identity free of the constraints of religion, of developing a culture based on Jewish values divorced from religious ritual. There were, on the other hand, those who regarded Zionism as the only way of preserving religious ritual in all its aspects, including the rebuilding of the Holy Temple and the revival of the sacrificial rites. Still others were content to work for the creation of an enlightened and just social democracy whose main concern would be the freedom, prosperity, and self-fulfillment of each individual.

One could fill volumes with descriptions of the querulous Zionist family and its trends and nuances, the panoply of love-hate relationships, the competitiveness, the use of covert influence, and the overt rivalry between its various components. Thus a rich texture of contrasts, complex and compelling, not only characterizes contemporary Israel, but was inherent in its very foundations. It may, of course, atrophy because of a superficial desire to "lower the fences" for the sake of unification around some trite common denominator. Or it may set off a violent, destructive explosion. But it may yet serve as a creative field of tension between various systems of values, as a sharp stimulus for cultural creativity through an intellectual and emotional struggle between differing visions. This will come if all of us accept pluralism not as a transient illness that must be eliminated, but as a blessing, and that we remember there are moments of truth when even a divided society must make a clear-cut decision on values and priorities.

A Moment of Truth

The occupation of the territories during the Six-Day War brought us to such a moment of truth. It forced Israel to make an operative decision on a question of theological, ideological, and moral dimensions. From behind the controversy over the future of the territories there peeked a far deeper question: What have we come here to be? The answer to that question, like other decisions, was postponed and repressed on the grounds that "Anyway, there's no one to talk to on the Arab side," and "We'll cross that bridge when we come to it." Since it seemed that the answer to the border question could wait ("until there's a phone call from the Arabs," as Moshe Dayan used to say), we avoided dealing with the problem of who we are, of what we have come here to be, which cannot be separated from the problem of the future of the territories, the purpose of the war, and the value of peace.

After that came the shock of the Yom Kippur War, which demanded an initial payment for this repression. This was followed by Sadat's visit and the peace treaty with Egypt, and then by the horror of Lebanon. There were certain indications of Arab willingness to accept Israel's existence (under conditions unacceptable to the majority of Israelis); at the same time, new ideologies sprang up concerning the advantage of Jewish life in the diaspora. Emigration became a mass phenomenon, and yet Israel continued to repress the question of the purpose and content of its existence, and to avoid decisions on its basic plans and blueprint. Instead, the controversy was focused on the shallow waters of the "limits of power," of what is "realistic" and what is not. It seems impossible to get to the question about our aims without first resolving the dilemma of the limits of power. Where does Israel's strength lie? What is its source? Can we rely on it indefinitely? We must discuss all this in order to pave the way for a discussion of who we are, what we want to be, and what our source of authority should be: the will of the people or the commandments of religious law.

The Limits of Power

The experience of power has intoxicated many of us, and understandably so: For thousands of years, the Jews gained experience in the power of faith and martyrdom, in economic, emotional, and intellectual powers, but they knew the power of physical force only from feeling it on their backs.

Now, all of a sudden, Jews have military power. Friend and foe are finally forced to take into account the physical strength of those whom they previously perceived as helpless. This is a new and dizzying experience, a test for which we may not be prepared and at which we may be failing now— even though, in fact, this power did not spring up suddenly, out of nowhere. It accumulated and was built up, line by line, acre by acre, gun by gun, over some one hundred years. It is the power that sprang from books and pamphlets, emerging from ethics, idealism, and self-sacrifice. It was created in the image of all these things. If the spirit that gave birth to this power should collapse, our physical strength would crumble and vanish.

It may be no surprise that a people who for thousands of years did not know how to maintain physical power should tend to become intoxicated with their newly discovered strength. It may be no surprise that many perceive physical power in simplistic and childish terms, without understanding the vital relationship between military strength and national potential, without understanding the connection between physical power and motivation, between motivation and moral strength, between moral strength and legitimacy or illegitimacy in the eyes of the international community, between that legitimacy and alliances with and support from other nations, and again—between alliances, support, and physical power.

In place of these subtleties there is a clamorous pull toward the clumsy, shallow theories of crude Darwinism, "catch as catch can," "dependence on others is a sin," and so on. Worse is the widespread blindness to the fatal connection between unceasing dependence on physical power, the arrogant display of might, the ritual of physical strength, on the one hand, and a surge of violence within our own society, on the other. One who teaches himself and his children to live by the crude principle that might makes right and that you should hold on tight to what you have grabbed, that victory is a sign of divine favor, that one who was once a victim is entitled to continue considering himself a victim even after he has turned others into victims, that life is "Slam, bam, thank you, ma'am"— he should not be surprised when these principles infiltrate the domestic fabric, relationships at work and between neighbors, family feelings, and even the line waiting at the bus stop.

Worst of all, perhaps, is the deceitful, demagogic tendency to redefine the aims of Zionism in accordance with the prospects offered by power—or that some people think it offers—to those who possess it. After the conquest of Beirut by the Israeli Army in 1983, voices were heard among the intellectual leadership of Gush Emunim urging us to use our weapons not just to defend ourselves, nor even just to turn Lebanon into an Israeli vassal state, but to "put the world right" and to force "the Jewish truth" on all Gentiles: "This war has proved to the entire world that there is only one military force in the Middle East that can be considered a superpower. Eradicating the nests of evil is only a preliminary process that will ultimately lead to the eradication of all evil in the world. The present reality has proved that the State of Israel is that force in the world" were the words of Rabbi Dov Lior, in *Seeds*.

The results of the war in Lebanon may have dampened these ecstasies somewhat. The thrill of "the Empire Strikes Back" may have waned a little. The debate over the limits of power was intended, as I have said, to silence and repress more deeply rooted controversies, such as the debate over the purpose of Zionism. And now, not long after Lebanon, the debate on the limits of power has been silenced as well, and not because the parties have reached agreement among themselves. We no longer ask: What can be achieved by power and what cannot? What is permitted and what is forbidden to accomplish by force? What is worth moving by force and what is not? What is the nature of force and what are its components?

Meanwhile, the power in our hands is twisting and corrupting us.

A Generation of Plainclothesmen and Military Governors

Ever since the days of the Book of Genesis there has been a struggle in Judaism between xenophobic tribalism ("with paeans to God in their throats and two-edged swords in their hands to wreak vengeance upon the nations") and an open, universalist attitude ("Are you not like the Ethiopians unto Me, O Children of Israel"). We must understand that both these approaches are authentically Jewish and that neither one is closer to "original" Judaism than the other. The Five Books of Moses, the ethics of the prophets, the literature of religious law and wisdom, and the collective creations of Jewish communities at various times and in various places reflect a primeval tension between these two basic attitudes toward the "outside world." This is the Dr. Jekyll and Mr. Hyde in Judaism.

Modern Zionism inherited this ambivalence. There, it has been expressed in conflicts, covert and overt, between the aspiration to be a "nation like all others," an attempt to become "like all the nations," and a lust to "pour out thy wrath upon the nations."

What began as a struggle for the right "to be a free people" evolved into an increasingly one-dimensional drive: to be free from foreign rule. But in the struggle many components of freedom were compromised for the sake of "freedom" to oppress others. In order to continue oppressing the Palestinians, we have been forced to sacrifice some of the hallmarks of a free nation, to sacrifice more and more in the area of individual freedom, to surrender to religious coercion and limitations of freedom in the name of security. Even freedom from dependence on strangers is turning, unwittingly, into subjugation to America. And the freedom a nation ruled by law grants to its citizens is becoming increasingly curtailed. "The law shall level mountains," we are told, "but not right now. For the time being, security must level the law."

The nation-state was created for the purpose of protecting life itself, says Aristotle, but the purpose of its existence is "the good life," that is, the realization of the personal and collective potential of the citizens of the state. In our country most of this potential is now being subordinated to the preservation of existence itself. This may be unavoidable. However, in recent years this potential has been increasingly enslaved to an obsession with expanded borders in the guise of preserving existence itself. Most of our creative energies are harnessed to swallowing up the occupied territories, to the exercise of an arrogant sovereignty, to a specious security that bears within it the seeds of its own destruction. A new generation of Israelis has come of age, a generation of soldiers, military governors, security forces, guards, and plainclothesmen. The state is drafting the flower of its manhood, not to defend itself, but to defend its "security belts." The state demands of its sons that they give their time, and sometimes their lives, for goals many of them regard as pointless and unrelated to the essential safeguarding of the state's survival. And meanwhile, day by day, before our very eyes, the famous "sociological pyramid" of Jewish existence is turning upside down, and the state that was born of the desire to transform the Jew from a social class into a nation is reducing us from a nation back to a social class.

Body and Soul

We do not have the power, in any constellation of circumstances, to defeat all the Arabs and to force upon them the attitude of "ancestral right" that is so sacred to some of us. We do not have the power to force the whole world to surrender to the will and appetite of some of us. We do not have the power to transform Dov Lior's fantasy into reality, namely, to "eradicate all evil from the world." We have only the power to choose whether or not to be evil ourselves.

The choice is, therefore, between compromise, agreement, and coexistence, on the one hand, and repeated attempts to bring about a decision by force on the other—with no assurance that our power will always be decisive, and with a profound fear of a process that will crumble the foundations of our strength. I do not contend that this choice is exclusively Israel's; it depends on the Arabs and on the superpowers, too. And it also depends on us, and on the goals, realistic or lunatic, that we set for ourselves.

The price of perpetual dependence, in the form of arms given to us, in part, by the generosity of others, the price of

79

the use of power to force the will of some of us upon the rest of the nation, upon the Palestinians, upon the world, may be unacceptably high. We are building our body on the ashes of our soul.

Davar, June 6, 1986

DEGREES OF EVIL

Mohammad, Gideon, and the Showers

Gideon Spiro, of Jerusalem, sent me the following letter, which I published, with minor deletions, in *Davar* in June 1987:

Jerusalem (within the Green Line)*

Dear Knesset Member:

I would like to bring to your attention the case of Mohammad Abu-Vardi, age twelve and a half, living at the Balata refugee camp near Nablus. On November 23, 1985, the Israeli Army conducted a search at the Balata refugee camp. At three o'clock that morning . . . the soldiers broke into the home of the Abu-Vardi family. . . . The soldiers woke the sleeping residents with shouts and kicks. . . . In their search, the soldiers found dangerous weapons in the form of five books on political subjects. . . . The three brothers were taken to the Fara'a

* Green Line: The armistice lines between Israel and its Arab neighbors, 1948–1967.

detention camp. . . . The interrogation of the boy of twelve and a half began the same day; it centered around the books. . . . A succession of beatings and tortures began. He was struck in the face and stomach. Afterward came a shower treatment (showers: does that remind you of anything?). From 4 P.M. until 11 P.M. Mohammad Abu-Vardi was taken to a cold shower each hour, and between one shower and the next he was interrogated in order to extract evidence from him against his brothers regarding the books. The interrogations were conducted amidst beatings while the boy was tied to a chair. . . . Other methods, too, were used in keeping with the brutal imagination of his sadistic interrogators. The boy screamed and wept, but to no avail. . . . The interrogation of Mohammad Abu-Vardi continued for twelve days. . . . The interrogations were accompanied by daily beatings. . . . Total period of detention: eighteen days.

Israel's poet laureate, Chaim Nachman Bialik (1873–1934), wrote, in his famous poem "On the Slaughter": "Not even the devil can invent a vengeance for the blood of a small child." In a slight variation one could say, "Not even the devil can find vengeance for a tortured Palestinian child." See what occupation and control over other people can do. The Israeli occupiers are turning into savage animals. . . . I am asking you to see that this case is investigated. . . . If you take no action, you will be an accomplice in this conspiracy of silence and cover-up. If you want to know where the next generation of Palestinian resistance to Israeli occupation is growing up, go to the detention centers in the occupied territories and you will find the answer. . . . Racism cannot be fought without plowing under the soil in which it grows. The occupation and the reality of apartheid which was created

from its loam are the fertilizer on which racism feeds. An
Israel that protects the torturers and murderers of children
. . . forfeits the right to judge war criminals who committed crimes against the Jewish people. . . .

So much for the gist of Gideon Spiro's letter. The following,
with minor deletions, is my reply:

1. I support the call for an investigation of the affair
reported in your letter.

2. You have not been quite fair to me: I am not a
member of the Knesset, nor am I a journalist. I have no
facilities to verify the story you have brought to my attention without having taken the trouble to indicate, even
by the slightest hint, the source of your story and how it
got to you.

3. I find several of the phrases in your letter abhorrent. In my eyes, anyone who indiscriminately refers to
the Israeli occupiers as "savage animals" is on a par with
those who call Palestinians "two-legged beasts" or
"cockroaches."

4. I am opposed to the continued Israeli occupation
of the populated Arab territories, but I reject the legiti-
mation that is inferred from your reference in your letter
to Arab terror as "Palestinian resistance." The so-called
Palestinian resistance never wasted its time on beating up
children. It concentrated on killing them indiscriminately, even before the Israeli occupation of the West
Bank and Gaza.

5. Your last sentence implies a comparison between
the Israeli occupiers and the Nazis. This comparison is
demagogic and perverted. The words "showers: does that

remind you of anything?" are truly obscene, unless you claim that the child was gassed to death, together with millions of other children, for the benefit of the Israeli soap industry.

6. As I have already stated, I support your call for an investigation, but I despise the crude, simplistic propagandist attitude that is reflected in almost every line of your letter, including the perverted association with the Nazis: the Israeli military government in the occupied territories is guilty of oppression, of intimidation, of torture, and of violating human rights, but the Palestinian "resistance" is guilty of a genocidal ideology and genocidal methods. The Nazis were not just people who beat up Jewish children in the course of confiscating books. Go do your homework.

To this, Gideon Spiro, of "Jerusalem (within the Green line)," replied:

You are angry at the mirror instead of the image. . . . I turned to you because I assumed that you are . . . an intellectual . . . a Jewish-Hebrew author with moral sensitivity . . . [who] would neither rest nor desist until the story . . . was thoroughly investigated. . . . Doesn't the phrase "savage animals" accurately reflect what was described here? . . . How many Jewish children have been killed by the Palestinian resistance in the territories occupied by Israel since 1967 and how many Palestinian children have been killed by the Israeli occupier since then? . . . The number of Palestinian and Lebanese children killed and wounded by Israeli bombings of Beirut, Tyre, Sidon, and the refugee camps is greater than all the Jewish casualties caused by the Palestinians since the coming of the first modern Zionist pioneers. . . . As one whose family fled from Germany five minutes before the outbreak of World War II, I am very cautious in expressing myself on this subject [the comparison with the Nazis]. . . . I reject the manipulative and demagogic use you make of shower torture that was employed by Israeli torturers against the Palestinian child. . . .

My reply to this letter from Gideon Spiro was approximately as follows:

With your permission, I would like to publish the Mohammad Abu-Vardi incident and the gist of our correspondence in *Davar*. This may be helpful in clarifying two issues: (1) the case of this child, and (2) whether it is possible to be, as you put it, an "author with moral sensitivity . . . with a belief in humanistic values . . ." etc., without identifying with what you term the "Palestinian resistance movement" and without justifying its methods and aims.

It seems to me that this question is pointless: General Raphael Eitan and Abu Nidal, Gush Emunim and Gideon Spiro all demand of us a black-and-white answer to: Who is the Nazi and who is the sacrificial lamb?

I don't buy this. The case of Mohammad Abu-Vardi, age twelve and a half, living at the Balata refugee camp must be investigated. If Spiro's claims are true, then those who tortured the child must be punished. But not by the laws enacted to deal with Nazi war crimes. It is forbidden to equate the shower in Nablus with the showers of Auschwitz. Anyone who makes such a comparison serves the aims that Meir Kahane and Muammar Qaddafi have in common. There are degrees of evil, and one who closes his eyes to that fact will eventually become the servant of evil. Such things have happened before.

NOTE: Following the publication of the above in *Davar*, Gideon Spiro wrote to me complaining that I had presented his second letter in a "filtered, chopped-up, and censored" fashion. Upon rereading the letter, I believe I have presented a fair summary of what he said. In two subsequent letters he wrote to me, Gideon Spiro claimed that I distorted his views and that "the comparison with the Nazis" does not express his attitude toward the Israeli occupation of Arab territory. I am pleased to hear that and I would bring what is written here to the attention only of those who irresponsibly continue to make comparisons with the Nazis in this regard. I regret that the editorial board of *Davar* did not respond to Spiro's request, which I supported, to publish our correspondence in its entirety.

POSTSCRIPT: Yitzhak Rabin, who was then the minister of Defense, wrote to me that the case of the child had been investigated by his office. According to him, Mohammad Abu-Vardi had never been arrested and the whole story was invented by PLO sources in East Jerusalem.

Peace via Morocco

During Shimon Peres's trip to Morocco, almost before the results of his talks were made public, reservations and sharp criticism were heard. Reservations were expressed by spokesmen for the nationalist right as well as by some of the moderates. According to spokesmen of the nationalist right, any talks with the Arabs endanger the Israeli hold on the territories, because the Arabs, including King Hassan of Morocco, demand all sorts of concessions from Israel. Better, then, that we should beware of "peace traps" of every kind and resume the "settlement momentum." Every Arab peace initiative must be met by an "appropriate Zionist response," until the Arabs lose all desire to talk peace with us, and the danger of peace ceases to rear its ugly head.

According to the critics of Peres among the moderates, talks with any Arab leader who is not in the PLO are misleading, contortionist, and a waste of precious time, since there can be no peace without the PLO.

Stereophonic Criticism

There is a fascinating resemblance between these constructs. Both of them reject the path through Morocco because it doesn't fit the inflexible, exclusive script written by each of these two schools of thought. Mrs. Geula Cohen, a right-wing nationalist, for instance, divides the Arabs approximately as follows. There is a species of Arab murderers who refuse to recognize Israel and who seek its destruction. With them, of course, we must have no contact. Distinct from these, she posits, there is a species of Arab murderers tainted by a characteristic sneakiness, who deceitfully profess a verbal willingness to come to terms with us under certain conditions, even though, in fact, they are thoroughly insincere. We must have no contact with that species either, because they are even more abominable than the other kind. They aren't merely murderers; they are sophisticated, honey-tongued murderers. In short, there is no one to talk to, and if there is, it only proves that there really isn't.

According to the version of some moderates, any Arab who is willing to talk peace with the wicked Israeli regime is a collaborator, and there's no point in talking with a collaborator. The only Arab worth talking to is an Arab who refuses to talk to us. It's like Groucho Marx refusing to join any club that would sink so low as to accept him as a member.

Despair

It is difficult to ignore the despair that echoes from both those approaches. Both of them maintain that the peace with Egypt is, at best, not particularly significant. Both are seeking to convince us that the only "authentic" Arab is the uninhibited terrorist. Both reject the path to peace via Morocco. Both assume that peace is possible only if Israel meets the most extreme Arab demand. One school adds: And therefore the meeting between King Hassan and Peres was a trap. The other school adds: Such attempts as the Hassan-Peres meeting are a waste of time and an illusion.

The Conflict Fades Away

Conflicts between peoples, like conflicts between individuals, almost never end with the discovery of some redemptive formula. Rather, they gradually fade away, from weariness, from a steady erosion of ideological commitment, from fear of the escalating price of the conflict, from a qualified willingness of the parties to make a half-conscious deal with their historical consciences. The ultimate "sacred" goal of each side is not renounced, but it gradually becomes a ritual thing to which lip service continues to be paid, both sides recognizing the sad necessity of leaving its fulfillment to some future generation.

Within the Arab world and among the Palestinians there are clear signs of weariness with the duration and the complications of the war to exterminate Israel. This should not be attributed to any "repentance" on the part of Arab ideologists, but to apprehensions about the price of a persistent attempt to "carry out justice to its fullest." According to a growing number of Arab spokesmen, that which was presented for all these years as a concrete goal, attainable within the foreseeable future, has come to be viewed as a utopian goal whose fulfillment has to be postponed until the end of days. A bitter irony can be seen in the fact that the very opposite process is happening in Israel: Many Israelis now see messianic goals as concrete objectives, attainable in our own time.

91

Disillusionment

Israel, therefore, also needs to go through a process of disillusionment, perhaps even two disillusionments. First, we must renew and expand our awareness that some of the old Zionist dreams that were rekindled by Israel's victory in the Six-Day War of 1967 are unattainable at this time, and that it is all right for the dreamers to postpone fulfillment until another day. Second, we must recognize that peace may come about gradually, in small steps, rather than by the scenario fancied by Israeli peace-seekers to the point where some of them are showing signs of addiction, unwilling to face any reality that does not conform to their exclusive scenario.

Shimon Peres's approach, within the constraints limiting him at every turn, is more realistic than that of those who reject the peace path via Morocco and insist on "all or nothing." A clear note of all or nothing resounds now from the arguments of people on both sides who attack the path to peace via Morocco.

Davar, June 15, 1986

The SCOUTS and the LADS

The rustle of pines, the mist around the towers on the mountain ridges, the ringing of church bells, the wail of the muezzin
at dawn, dusk descending upon the spires of the city walls and
on the gold- and silver-domed mosques, dappled alleyways,
undulating terraces of olive groves—these are all parts of the
cliché Jerusalem in literature and in nostalgia. For brevity's
sake we will use the acronym of the words "spires, church
bells, olive groves, undulating terraces" and, in this essay, refer
to Jerusalemites who are addicted to the ambience of their city
as described by the cliché as SCOUTS.

Between the War of Independence in 1948 and the Six-
Day War in 1967, when Jerusalem was physically divided, the
SCOUTS would longingly hug to themselves memories of the
long-lost charms of a Jerusalem united under British rule. But
then, immediately after the Six-Day War, they were seized by
a sudden nostalgia for the divided Jerusalem of the days before
1967.

The British Golden Age had been destroyed, it seemed,

by the partition of the city in 1948, whereas the removal of the barbed-wire fences in 1967 turned the period of the divided city into a sort of retroactive golden age. So within twenty years the SCOUTS had suffered the destruction of the first and second Temples all over again.

No wonder the SCOUTS generally tend to appear melancholy.

The View from Tel Aviv

Conscientious Tel Avivians have always shown a certain aversion toward melancholy Jerusalem in all its modern reincarnations. The pioneers of Tel Aviv seventy years ago viewed Ottoman Jerusalem as a decaying Levantine ghetto. Fifty years ago, in the view from Tel Aviv, British Jerusalem appeared to be a self-conscious, isolated city, snobbish, nonpioneering, un-Israeli, and completely incapable of participating in the uninhibited festivities of Tel Aviv street carnivals. During the period between the War of Independence and the Six-Day War, Tel Aviv perceived the divided city of Jerusalem as a backwater, sleepy, dreary, and provincial. Today, Jerusalem appears to Tel Avivians to be a fanatical loony bin—Israel's twin to the Iranian city of Qom, the threatening stronghold of the dark forces of Khomeinism in Israel, with all the covert and overt meaning the LADS of Tel Aviv attach to the term "dark." (LADS here and hereafter refers to the Learned Ashkenazi Dovish Secularists.)

The Juniyeh-Qom Highway

The Tel Aviv LADS, especially in recent years, no longer feel any admiration for the Jerusalem SCOUTS. The days are gone when the LADS (and the LASSIES) would make the pilgrimage to Jerusalem during their years of romantic soul-searching in order to acquire scouting "experience," and then to "descend" (or not) from the sacred to the profane. But today the SCOUTS, for the most part, are also LADS. The distinction between them, therefore, is neither simple nor clear nowadays. In any event, the Jerusalem SCOUTS have begun to join the Tel Aviv LADS in their disgust for "the stronghold of the forces of darkness." There is still some dispute between LADS and SCOUTS on how to evaluate the past (did Jerusalem, or did it not, have some ineffable charms in its previous incarnations?). However, there is wide agreement today between SCOUTS and LADS when it comes to the present and the future: Regardless of whether Jerusalem has a past worth longing for, it certainly has no future. Moreover, in the eyes of SCOUTS and LADS alike, the Jerusalem of today is the epitome of the Israeli scene in the 1980s. It poses a Khomeinistic threat to Tel Aviv and the entire country.

Thus, the rapprochement between SCOUTS and LADS is a result of the fall of Jerusalem to the forces of darkness. Some say that a not insignificant number of SCOUTS are now packing their bags and heading for the highway that runs from Qom to Juniyeh* to seek political asylum, as it were, on the banks of Tel Aviv's Yarqon River. And sociologists will point out, of course, that the prophecy of the destruction of Jerusalem is self-fulfilling.

------

* Juniyeh: a Christian suburb of Beirut notorious for its "dolce vita" during the Lebanese War while Christian forces were being battered by their Moslem enemies.

Sepia Picture Postcards and New Clichés

Let us take another brief moment for a peek at the images and clichés already tattered from overuse. The SCOUTS, for example, depicted British Jerusalem, in and out of literature, as a cosmopolitan, dreamy, meditative entity, the permanent arena for oh-so-European tea parties, trinational salon conversations on morality, history, mysticism, and philosophy. Through the window of the philosophizing trinational tea drinkers one could always see, without exception, the desert, the domes and minarets, one or two prophets of doom, a moonstruck Christian crusader, an olive tree, a dervish, and a cave, and hear a muezzin and the ringing of bells in the background.

Those who were enchanted by this picture postcard viewed Tel Aviv with an air of cold, aristocratic condescension. They perceived Tel Aviv as a shallow steam bath, hurried and noisy, a little like a shtetl, petit-bourgeois, somewhat bohemian in a vulgar way, somewhat working-class with pseudo-proletarian pretensions. In short, a hick town, shrill, ugly, and very, very plebeian.

The LADS, on the other hand, continue to feel nostalgia for the sepia picture postcard showing a young, vibrant Tel Aviv, a city of painters, experimental theater, workers' councils, and a former professor from Berlin selling hot dogs at the Mugrabi cinema.

Clearly, the LADS thought that the Jerusalem of the SCOUTS had never existed except as a sort of folk-art souvenir.

The little album through which we have just leafed, an exhibition of four cliché postcards—Jerusalem as seen by the SCOUTS, Tel Aviv as seen by the SCOUTS, Tel Aviv as seen by the LADS, and Jerusalem as seen by the LADS—is all part of the past. New clichés, freshly baked by both SCOUTS and LADS, are now quickly produced and distributed: Tel Aviv is perceived now as the last stronghold of the remains of "sane Israel," an enlightened, tolerant, broad-minded island amid a torrent of savagery and zealotry. Jerusalem is painted as the heart of darkness; Jerusalem has fallen to the "obscurantists."

Perhaps we'd better deal with these clichés before they get out of hand.

Tel Aviv: The Mea Shearim of the Dovish Left?

Who, in the final analysis, are the forces of obscurantism? Are they the black-coated, anti-Zionist, ultra-Orthodox Jews in the Mea Shearim quarter* who maintain contact with the PLO and put their trust in it? Or the students of the militant, nationalistic Rabbinical schools who dream of replacing the State of Israel with the Kingdom of Israel? Are they the bearded young Islamic zealots from the Arab quarters? Or the riffraff of Meir Kahane? Or the worshipers at the Western Wall? Or the Soviet immigrants, of whom not a few are at the extreme right of the political spectrum? Or the affluent immigrants from Western countries who buy fancy homes in the Old City and in the artists' quarter, maintain an English-speaking enclave in Jerusalem, and tend to support the right in general and the religious right in particular? Or the ultra-Orthodox Sephardic religious neighborhoods that provide recruits for Rabbi Peretz's Shas party? Or maybe the obscurantists are the masses of fans of Jerusalem's Betar soccer team? Or the vo-

---

* Mea Shearim, one of the first Jewish neighborhoods built outside the walls of the Old City of Jerusalem (in 1874), is a stronghold of ultra-Orthodoxy.

ciferous community of religious repentents? Or the Lubavitcher Hassidim, or their rivals, the Hassidim of Satmar, or
the Hassidim of Ger? Or the dovish followers of Rabbi Eliezer
Shach? Or the ardent supporters of Ariel Sharon?

It seems the LADS of Tel Aviv make no distinctions among
all these. To them, it is all a scary, sickening "mixed grill."
To them, it is all one ferocious shadow, a dark storm that has
inundated Jerusalem and now threatens to spill over, down
the slopes of the Judean hills, sweeping over Tel Aviv, which
is depicted in this cliché as a besieged Masada of Ashkenazi-
dovish-intellectual secularism.

The sin and folly of the LADS (and of the SCOUTS that
follow in their footsteps) are, first and foremost, their lack of
all curiosity, their indolence toward making distinctions, their
refusal to face the adversary, their nurturing of a ghetto mentality on the banks of the Yarqon. The term "dark ones" or
"forces of darkness," when used by LADS and SCOUTS, reeks of
ethnic condescension and intellectual arrogance. But most of
all, it emits a stench of panic. When viewing the stranger as
faceless, one comes to see oneself as a beleaguered minority
surrounded by enemies. Geula Cohen and her right-wing supporters frequently accuse the intellectual Israeli left of defeatism because of its willingness to compromise on the question
of borders. This accusation is based on malice and narrow-
mindedness. But there is, in a completely different sense, a
defeatist chord in the positions of the LADS and the SCOUTS:
Their siege mentality is defeatist. Their tendency to declare
that all is lost, that Israel is falling to the obscurantists now,
if it hasn't already fallen, is defeatist. Their self-image of a
marginal minority, persecuted and helpless, a label they wear
with a kind of coquettish loser's pride, is defeatist. In short,
swelling tones of hysteria tempered with self-pity have been

increasingly heard of late from the territory of "sane and balanced Israel."

Condescension and lack of curiosity: South of Bat Yam, north of Ramat Aviv, east of Tel Hashomer, just past metropolitan Tel Aviv, the country is pictured as occupied by the "dark obscurantists." Is there life after Bugrashov Street?

Enchanting, shabby Tel Aviv, so secular and melancholy. A ragged and sexy city, sensuous, bourgeois, bohemian, and poor, whose eyes cloud over when she gazes at Jerusalem, seeing nothing but a "dark" athletic rapist closing in on her. Skits destroy her with satire. Her theaters and newspapers, her poets and comedians, in hedonistic self-indulgence, are acting out the Last Days of Pompeii and the Ship of Fools, in an intoxicating, wondrous wave of desperate creative energy, of wit and self-pity. It is now five minutes before midnight, Tel Aviv time.

Isn't this almost comical? Jerusalem, preoccupied with itself, is in no way about to flood the coastal plain of Tel Aviv. The "dark ones" are less of a monolith than the LADS and the SCOUTS. Much less. The new Jerusalem cliché and Tel Aviv's new self-image are both tainted with shallow, stereotypic vapidity, no less than previous incarnations of the clichés of Jerusalem and Tel Aviv.

The Dark Ones Are Coming, the Dark Ones Are Coming

Only they aren't coming anywhere, except perhaps to the cabarets of Tel Aviv, staging a thousand variations on the melodrama of the destruction of sane Tel Aviv by "the forces of darkness." Tel Aviv glorifies its sanity and dreads the foes of sanity—as though that sanity were a virginal hymen to be

99

protected against lusting hordes. So much so that it sometimes seems that behind the fortifications of "sanity," or, should we say, beneath the well-girded chastity belt, there lurks at last the faint beginning of mild insanity.

The bald truth is that right now within "dark" Jerusalem desperate spiritual, political, and religious battles are being fought—fiercer and more fateful than those waged between the representatives of various nuances of the LADS' civilization. For instance, there is an abyss that divides the nonnationalist ultra-Orthodox zealots from the ultra-nationalist Orthodox zealots. If the apparatus of the nation-state were suddenly to disappear, there might be pitched battles between Gush Emunim and Mea Shearim, not to mention the depth of alienation and contempt between the Hassidim and the Mitnagdim,* between one band of Hassidim and another band of Hassidim, between one faction of Mitnagdim and another faction of Mitnagdim. And, much more important, there is the deep chasm that divides all these types of Orthodoxy from the stormy hedonistic vitality of the Middle East, secular to its core, demonstrated by the masses of Jerusalem's soccer fans. And there is the gap between all three of these groups and the "Anglo-Saxon" bourgeois enclave that has sprung up in Jerusalem. And the gap that separates all four of these from Arab Jerusalem, which is also characterized by deep rifts, including the rift between Europeanized nationalist radicals and Moslem zealots. And so on, and so forth.

All of this completely escapes the frightened, clouded eyes of the LADS of Tel Aviv.

So it would seem that precisely the depth of these internal contrasts among various kinds of Jerusalemites may guarantee

* The Mitnagdim are non-Hassidic Jews.

pluralism in Israel, and, with it, the survival of "Tel Avivan civilization."

Signing Sight Unseen

If the right were to nominate Ariel Sharon, for example, to succeed Teddy Kollek as mayor of Jerusalem, we can assume he would lose, because the "Kollek coalition" would defeat him: the ultra-Orthodox (with the exception of Gush Emunim and its supporters), the SCOUTS, and the Arabs would band together against him.

If the ultra-Orthodox were to nominate an ultra-Orthodox religious leader, say Rabbi Yitzhak Peretz, for mayor, we can assume, again, that a coalition of SCOUTS, Gush Emunim, Hassidim, and Arabs, together with the Betar soccer fans, would defeat him.

Perhaps this is sufficient to dispel the simplistic Tel Avivan cliché about a "united Khomeinist front," which supposedly reigns in Jerusalem and threatens to overrun the Tel Avivan fortress of sanity.

But the LADS now tend to avoid reflection, and thereby differences and nuances, and instead prefer generalizations: "Anyone who is different from us is a threat to us," "They're all exactly the same," "Don't trust them," "They're all animals," or "It's them or us, there can be no compromise between them and us." Comfortable padded slogans like these almost constitute a parallel nowadays between our primitive right and the primitive attitude of some Tel Avivan LADS toward the right. The same style is used by many right-wing Israeli hawks when they tell us that "all Arabs are the same." More and more, this style characterizes the attitude of the doves toward the "dark ones." The phrase used by the Gush Emunim

101

rabbinic leaders, "Israel is the lamb surrounded by a pack of wolves," is almost the twin of "a sane Tel Aviv surrounded by the local Hezbollah," the pet phrase of many LADS and LASSIES on the banks of the Yarqon. Sometimes the two rub shoulders in the weekend editions of the afternoon newspapers, and if you replace "dark ones" with "Arabs," you can almost replace a byline from the right with one from the left. Both sides apparently need the intoxicating drug of being a handful of besieged heroes, the "last defenders of the walls." Both sides try to avoid sorting, grading, and differentiating when speaking of their "worst enemies." One will tell you to cut out the nonsense about the presumed nuances between Arafat and Abu Nidal, between Sadat and Qaddafi. The other will tell you to cut out the nonsense about the presumed nuances between Meir Kahane and the National Religious party, or between Ariel Sharon and Yitzhak Rabin. Both sides go blithely forward with their eyes closed; they've already seen more than enough. They've heard more than enough. Don't confuse them with additional facts. They'll sign, sight unseen, anything that says the bad guys out there have sworn to destroy us. And that's the way it is.

Nevertheless, the Danger Is Real

It is true—a temporary, very dangerous coalition of most of the forces of darkness is possible in Israel. The widespread resentment toward "Western culture," the contempt for democracy, the hostility toward openness, permissiveness, and toward the spirit of criticism, hatred of the Arabs, of intellectuals, and of the left, plus indifference—if not worse—toward the principles of law and the authority of the Knesset may all come together one day in a coalition that would put an end to the State of Israel in its present form, and certainly shatter our hopes of creating an open, just, and more democratic Israel. There is no doubt that this danger exists. Such things have been known to happen.

Yet precisely these frightening political possibilities should move us to cool, clearheaded political reflection, rather than drive us into a foaming, desperate panic and hysteria. (Several months ago I counted, in one single issue of the left-wing magazine *Haolam HaZeh*, no fewer than sixteen comparisons between what happened in Germany just before Hitler's rise to power and what took place in Israel that week. The issue included one story about an unfortunate man who was convicted by a court of justice and vociferously expressed an opinion about the profession of the judge's mother. The magazine indicated that just such an incident had occurred in Germany shortly before the Nazi takeover. No less.) In this matter, too, it would be hard to refrain from pointing out that the extremely hawkish right and the extremely sane and balanced left are both developing an increasing dependence on the Nazi precedent. The right-wing journalist Eliahu Amikam, writing in *Yediot Aharonot*, places the present State of Israel in Warsaw, right in the middle of the Jewish ghetto, between one deportation transport and the next. On the other side of the very same op-ed page of that newspaper my friend Boaz Evron puts us on the "Aryan side" of the Nazi metaphor, making comparisons not between ourselves and those who were transported to the gas chambers, but between ourselves and those who did the transporting. In both instances, the writer enlists the Nazis in order to sharpen his argument, for the sake of simplification, and to make that luscious cry of *Gewalt*.

The New Class

If we can succeed in wiping out the panic over the "dark peril that is upon you, Tel Aviv," and propose in its place a levelheaded view vis-à-vis the forces of darkness, we may discover that the most exciting and widespread political, cultural, social, and religious phenomenon that has occurred in Israel in the last fifteen or twenty years has been, not nationalist extremism, and certainly not "repentant" religious fundamentalism, but, rather, the emergence and growing prominence of a new middle class, mostly Sephardic, a class that already appears to comprise about one-third of Israel's population. This is a class that already seems to hold the key to every major political change in Israel, a class that already seems to be aware of its own weight and decisive political power. It is a class that already seems to have opted unambiguously for a secular, Western life-style (with a very thin veneer of "Jewish traditionalism") and seems to have rejected, quietly but firmly, the Orthodox way of life. A class that already seems to have decided, quietly but categorically, against the option of a "return to its Oriental roots." A class that, in great numbers, rejected the religious educational system, choosing to send its children to secular academic and vocational public schools instead. A class that, in great numbers, rejected the temptation (including attractive material benefits, such as subsidized housing, etc.) to settle in the heart of the occupied territories, and spurned the invitation of the ultra-Orthodox to give up pork chops, pop singers, and various and sundry other Mediterranean delights.

This new class (stated in broad generalization) is rather hawkish, but it is far removed from messianic fanaticism. It is somewhat "traditional," but it is very selective in its decisions

about which religious commandments to observe and which—
and this comprises the majority of the commandments—to
ignore. It is a public whose taste, life-style, tendencies, and
preferences impart a clearly Mediterranean flavor to Israel.
With each passing day, Israel moves farther and farther away
from Theodor Herzl's fantasy, the replication of the Austria-
Hungary of Emperor Franz Josef in the heart of the Middle
East. But it also moves farther and farther away from the
fundamentalist life-style of Khomeini and the Hezbollah, from
a "Torah state," the "Kingdom of the Messiah." Israel is becoming a warmhearted, Mediterranean country, loud, tem-
peramental, hearty; not too different from the character
sometimes ascribed to Greece, Spain, or Italy (including certain aspects that frighten those Jews whose parents came from
Warsaw or those who ache to turn Israel into the image of
what they saw and worshiped during their most recent sab-
batical in Oxford or in Boston).

Nevertheless, cautious reflection may reveal to us, among
other things, that this new middle class, which is the center
ring of Israel now, is far from being a threat to democracy or
a mortal danger to the world of the LADS of Tel Aviv or the
SCOUTS of Jerusalem. On the contrary, it appears to be democratic, if not anarchistic to the bone: "No one's gonna tell
me what to do. Shimon Peres is nuts. Yitzhak Shamir is out
of his mind. Those rightists are crazy. Those leftists have gone
too far" (or vice versa). In comparison with equivalent social
groups in Western countries, the new Israeli middle class is
quite tolerant. And it certainly doesn't desire the destruction
of the civilization of the Tel Avivan LADS. Quite the opposite:
It is influenced by that civilization, attracted to it, and has
even adopted some of its treasures.

That is our center ring. In relation to that ring, both the

rabbis of Gush Emunim and the radical playwrights of Tel Aviv are the outer fringe.

An Alliance?
Perhaps, But It Won't Be Easy

There is no reason for rejoicing over the aspirations, preferences, tastes, and political tendencies of the new Israeli middle class. Simplification, populism, power worship, and hatred of Arabs are no less widespread in its ranks than contempt for intellectuals and ridicule for "do-gooders." I did not write the above lines as a serenade to this new class. I meant to examine it and to attempt to offer SCOUTS and LADS an assessment of the situation, arguing that not all is lost. The "battle for Jerusalem" has not yet been decided. There is no sensible explanation for the impulse of the SCOUTS and LADS to put up their own tombstone and compose a requiem and an epitaph for themselves.

Above all, there is no justification or logic whatsoever for the tendency to use the expression "forces of darkness" to describe hundreds of thousands of Israelis whose parents, twenty or thirty years ago, may have spent their Sabbaths at the synagogue but who, in our day, have voted with their feet—or with their cars—in favor of a Sabbath spent on the beach or at a barbecue in the park.

It is quite possible that in some future constellation of circumstances these will be allies (though not necessarily comfortable ones) in the struggle for a secular, open, and self-critical image of Israel. Indeed, it may be possible, under certain conditions, to find allies within this new class even in the struggle over an Israeli withdrawal from the populated Arab areas of the West Bank and the Gaza Strip.

If Jerusalem Were No More

The panic-stricken LADS do not see the situation this way. What would happen, they ask themselves, if Jerusalem were no more? (Answer: We would pull back to Tel Aviv. In Tel Aviv, among ourselves, among our own kind, we'll feel nice and warm.) And what if Tel Aviv should fall? (Projected answer: Then we'll have to prepare ourselves for a life as homeless people. Here and there we can already find some Rabbi Yohanan Ben Zakkai laying, perhaps, the preliminary foundations for a Yavneh of SCOUTS and LADS, a Yavneh on the banks of the Hudson, where the remnants of the LADS will flee to set up a Hebrew "spiritual center" for the time after the fall of Jerusalem and Tel Aviv.)* This, too, may turn out to be a self-fulfilling prophecy. There are some LADS who, as early as 1967, invested their emotional and intellectual capital in a stock called the "Nazification of Israel." In 1967, this was a very esoteric stock. Its value rose steadily in the market with the institutionalization of the Israeli occupation of the West Bank and Gaza, the rise of nationalism, and the corruption, as an occupying power, of Israeli society. In 1973, with the Yom Kippur War, the value of the Nazification of Israel stock doubled, and doubled again with the rise of the right to power in 1977. It skyrocketed once more after the filthy war in Lebanon, the emergence of Kahanism, and the murder of Emil Grunzweig. The establishment of the Shamir-Peres government in 1984, the withdrawal from Lebanon, the stabilization of the economy, and the slowdown of the nationalist-racist wave seem to have caused a slight drop in the value of this

* After the destruction of the Second Temple by the Romans, in A.D. 20, the small town of Yavneh, south of Jaffa, became the focus of Jewish religious and spiritual life. Yavneh symbolizes the moderate, realistic, and submissive trends in Judaism.

stock: the "Nazi" wave has ebbed somewhat. Perhaps it is only human that the stockholders, people who believe that the worse things get, the better, reacted angrily to the establishment of the Shamir-Peres government and the achievements of its first two years. Rabbi Yohanan Ben Zakkai, who had fled from Jerusalem in the dark of night (during the first century C.E.), with his books and a handful of disciples, to Yavneh to save the spiritual treasures of his people from the calamity brought down on Jerusalem by the Zealots, surely must have felt a little embarrassed when he turned on his transistor radio one bright morning in Yavneh, only to hear—how embarrassing, outrageous!—that the Zealots no longer reigned in Jerusalem, and that there were even indications of de-escalation and the opening of peace negotiations. This development now upsets the Yavneh plan and may devalue the Nazi stock. If, despite everything, there is still Jerusalem, then the position (both emotional and intellectual) of those who invested their capital (both emotional and intellectual) in a doomsday scenario will be embarrassing, outrageous, and—who knows?—maybe even a little ridiculous.

Phalanges in Reverse

The term Phalangist is derived from the Greek word "phalanx." The phalanx, in the Greek and Roman armies, was a unique battle formation. The soldiers were arranged in a closed-square formation, their backs to one another and their faces turned toward an enemy who could neither outflank nor surprise them, because in this formation the men gave full cover to one another in every direction. The lances and spears pointed outward, of course, in all four directions.

The moderate, dovish Israeli left sometimes resembles a reverse phalanx: a square of brave fighters, their backs to the whole world and their faces and their sharpened, unsheathed pens turned on one another. I do not mean to minimize the importance of mutual criticism, the clarification of nuances, the vital struggle over the essence of the positions the dovish left should adopt. But it seems that the civil wars among the LADS are swallowing up almost all our political energy. Perhaps this, too, bears witness to the deep flaw mentioned before— the lack of genuine interest in the true adversary and the lack of genuine enthusiasm for the struggle that is, after all, the true struggle. We had better turn around, face outward, and discern nuances, differentiate between deep dark and light dark, for example, and, most important, differentiate between darkness and dark moods.

Like children frightened by the very creature they had invented, we have been overcome by hysteria over the myth of the "united forces of darkness." Except for the eyes of the SCOUTS and the LADS, almost everything in Jerusalem is still open. And almost everything, including the worst and including the not-so-awful, is still possible.

Davar Hashavua, May 22, 1987

On Degrees of Evil

In January 1986, the International PEN Congress convened in New York. The theme of the congress was "The Imagination of the State and the Imagination of the Writer." Many speeches were given in the spirit of romantic anarchism, namely, declaring that the state, any state, is a monster that tramples the spirit of the simple individual—who is by nature good—with wars, oppression, and the construction of ugly housing projects. Writers, on the other hand, were depicted as courageous people who come out in opposition to the monstrous state to defend the "little man." The following address was delivered in response to these speeches.

The state has no imagination. "The imagination of the state" exists only in the imagination of some writers, like those who invented the title of this congress. St. George and the Dragon— something like that must have been on their minds when they contrived this title. Every writer an empty-handed Solzhenitsyn, every dragon a wicked Leonid Brezhnev or a vicious Richard Nixon. I don't like it. I think some states are relatively decent. So are some writers. And some states and some writers are corrupt in many different ways. Our title has about it a ring of romantic, simplistic anarchism. I reject the image of a saintly lot of writers marching fearlessly to combat heartless bureaucracies on behalf of all the sweet and simple human beings out there. I am not in the business of the beauties versus the beasts.

For one thing, states and governments and bureaucracies—the fair ones *and* the hideous ones; there are both— have always been inspired by all sorts of visions generating from all kinds of writers. Some of these visions are fair, some are bad, some are monstrous—visions that various rulers have or have not distorted in ways that different writers have condemned. Or praised.

For another, some writers have indeed died in jails and gulags while some others have thrived in courts and dachas. But most have neither died in martyrdom nor thrived by licking boots. None of us has ever killed a dragon. Moreover, the sweet and simple common people out there are neither sweet nor simple. We know, most of us, better than that. Just read our books and see.

Again and again I am amazed by the gulf between what writers see when we write our poems, stories, plays, and what we do when we formulate or sign our petitions, manifestos, titles for panel discussions. It is as if we were using two contradictory pairs of eyes—present company not excluded; myself not excluded. Most of us know a thing or two about the dragons inside the human heart. Yet outside our literary works we often tend to sound as if we believe in the simplistic, dangerous, Rousseauistic assumption that governments and establishments are wicked—all of them—whereas common people are born pure and sweet in heart—all of them.

I beg to differ. The state is a necessary evil simply because many individuals are themselves capable of evil. Moreover, there are differences among states. Some are almost good, some are bad, some are lethal. And since writers are, or at least they ought to be, in the subtleties department and in the precision department, it is our job to differentiate. Whoever ignores the existence of varying degrees of evil is bound to become a servant of evil.

Precision and subtleties—we are not reporters, and yet we are. We do not necessarily collect or reflect facts; we invent, we twist, we exaggerate, we distort. We turn things inside out and upside down. But note: The moment we put things into words, our words are promoted into evidence. Hence our responsibility for precision, for nuances, for subtleties. Hence our duty to map evil, to grade it, to measure its degrees.

The tragedy of history is not the perpetual hopeless clash between saintly individuals and diabolical establishments. It is, rather, the perpetual clash between the relatively decent societies and the bloody ones. To be more precise, it is the perpetual cowardice of relatively decent societies whenever they confront the ruthlessness of oppressive ones.

How can one be humane, which means skeptical and capable of moral ambivalence, and at the same time try to combat evil? How can one stand fanatically against fanaticism? How can one fight without becoming a fighter? How can one struggle against evil without catching it? Deal with history without becoming exposed to the poisonous effect of history? Three months ago, in Vienna, I saw a street demonstration of environmentalists protesting against scientific experiments on guinea pigs. They carried placards with images of Jesus surrounded by suffering guinea pigs. The inscription read: "He loved them too." Maybe he did, but some of the protesters looked to me as if eventually they may not be above shooting hostages in order to bring an end to the sufferings of the guinea pigs. Which is, to some extent, the story of do-gooders here and there, and maybe everywhere.

Let us not ascribe a demonic imagination to the state and a redeeming imagination to ourselves. Let us not give in to the temptation of simplification. We ought to be telling the bad from the worse from the worst.

The New Republic, February 24, 1986

MESSIAH NOW, AMALEK NOW

The Source of Authority

The attempt to burn a synagogue in a suburb of Tel Aviv was truly a despicable act, and it aroused gruesome memories. The placing of sexually provocative billboards in religious neighborhoods is an act of insensitivity. And some of the recent reactions from secular Jews are indeed warped by gross generalizations.

But the appeal from the president of the state and others, calling on "both sides" to act with restraint, or to "build a bridge across the stormy waters," was insulting and unjust: Most of the religious public and almost all of the secular public have thus far taken law-abiding, nonviolent positions in the dispute between them.

Love of Zion and Guilt of Samaria

There are small groups of ultra-Orthodox Jews who have never recognized the Zionist state and its laws. These groups, whether in Mea Shearim, Bnei Brak, or among Gush Emunim and its followers, benefit from the Zionist entity; they receive budgetary allocations, protection, services, and security even while refusing to recognize its authority over them. In their eyes there is no sovereign except the Sovereign of the Universe.

The wisdom of generations taught these believers forbearance and compromise, to defer the supremacy of Torah until the coming of the final Redemption, and, in the meantime, to live in a flawed reality and to wait with perfect faith, without forcing the issue, for salvation from heaven.

It seems that the establishment of the "heretical Zionist state" shattered their patience. An obsession with the Messiah has awakened, almost simultaneously, in various corners of the believer camp. Disciples of the rabbis Kook—father and son—imagined they heard the stirrings of the Messiah in the roar of the tanks during the Six-Day War. And now the dybbuk has spread to other fringes of Halakic Judaism. The right-wing Jewish settlers in Sebastia, through violence and threats of a rift, managed to bring the Rabin government to its knees in 1977. Now other religious factions are seeking to bring the Peres government to its knees by similar methods, including the establishment of an underground commando force and organizing themselves to destroy the rule of law even as they issue whining, self-righteous threats much like those of Gush Emunim: "Accept all of our dictates, or you will be responsible for a split across the nation."

Even the statements issued by the president, the attorney general, and other peacemakers recall the tumultuous days of Samaria: Under no circumstances will we give in to violence, but if the violence is stopped, we will do everything in our power to meet the demands of those who started it. In other words: We will tolerate neither the burning of bus stops nor other kinds of lawlessness, but we will grant the arsonists their wishes if only they stop setting fires.

The people who demand my wallet at knife point will

not receive it until they put away the knife; then they will get what they want. And peace and status quo upon the House of Israel.

Autonomy for Persons or Places?

The real problem is that there are some religious Jews who do not and cannot accept any law except rabbinic law. The heart of the problem is a question of the source of authority: Are the people sovereign, through the Knesset and its laws, or is there no sovereign other than the Sovereign of the Universe, no law other than the law of Torah?

The problem can be papered over for the sake of domestic peace. It can be delayed. It can be repressed. But it cannot be eliminated. The problem is solely for the religious public to tackle, inasmuch as virtually all secular Jews have accepted, and will continue to accept, sometimes with clenched teeth, all the laws enacted by the Knesset—including laws passed due to coalition pressures and shady deals. At most, some of them will be pushed to a sense of internal exile.

The religious public, however, stands at a crossroad. They will have to make up their minds: either the messianic era has already arrived and the time has come to shove rabbinic law down the throat of a majority that does not want it, or else the messianic era has not yet arrived, and they will have to go on praying, believing, and waiting.

If widespread sectors of the religious community believe that the Messiah is at the gate, then no compromise is possible and there is, from their point of view, no room for tolerance and forbearance. In that case, there is no choice for the secular Zionist majority but to grant full autonomy to the religious people and to the limited territories in which there is such a messianic majority: the right of self-determination to the point

117

of secession, for both the ultranationalist religious Jewish set-
tlers in Hebron and the anti-Zionist ultra-Orthodox Jews in
Mea Shearim and some other neighborhoods. Messianic logic
leads to a partition of the land, not just between Jews and
Palestinians, but between libertarian Zionist Jews and those
Jews who cannot accept the people as the source of authority,
sovereignty, and law. Thus let there be a Zionist state for the
Zionists and, alongside it—under conditions of peace and se-
curity—a Palestinian state for the Palestinians, an ultra-
Orthodox state for the ultra-Orthodox, and a settlers' state for
the settlers of Gush Emunim. In the words of American poet
Robert Frost, "Good fences make good neighbors."

Messiah Now or the Unity of Israel?

The option of separation and secession is infinitely better than
the danger of continuous civil strife. The reality of partition
is preferable, in every respect. The secular Zionist public
which is ready to separate peacefully from the Palestinians
should not be frightened by the idea of establishing one or two
ultra-Orthodox Jewish "Vatican Cities," a few dozen acres
each, nor by the idea of autonomy for Gush Emunim settlers
within a zone of Palestinian autonomy. The division is a sad
fact, and the separation will be no more than an honest expression of this division: We will not obtrude ourselves on anyone
who is unwilling or incapable of being Israeli because Israel
is too Jewish for him, or not Jewish enough—in short, anyone
who feels that a Zionist, democratic Israel conflicts with his
principles. A Zionist, democratic Israel will be able, under
certain conditions, to exist and even to flourish alongside an
independent Palestine, an autonomous Torahland, and an
autonomous settlerland. We are not thinking, heaven forbid,
about dispossession, exile, deportation, or ghettoization. We

118

are talking about granting a piece of land for self-determination and self-fulfillment to whoever feels he has not attained self-determination and fulfillment within the State of Israel: to the Palestinian who will not settle for anything less than the total actualization of his nationalism, and to the Jew who will not settle for anything less than a total reign of Torah. It is fascinating to contemplate that if Israel were to disappear suddenly, the Palestinians might immediately jump at one another's throats even as the various Orthodox Jewish sects would be drawn into ferocious confrontation over the form of the rabbinic government they so fervently desire. Nevertheless, there is no reason for a Zionist state to take upon itself the role of bouncer in a hall full of groups that unanimously wish that the bouncer would disappear. Thus, the question lies before the religious public: Do you want a theocratic government ruling over tiny, scattered pieces of territory, or coexistence at the price of giving up the realization of a rabbinic regime? Messiah Now at the price of severance from the House of Israel, or acceptance of the secular democratic principle by which the people are the ultimate sovereign, the source of law and authority through the instruments of Knesset and legislation?

The question is a religious, a theological one. Let us not relate to it as if it were a question of policing. Let the religious public and its spiritual leaders give us their answer, one way or the other.

Davar, June 23, 1986

119

Amalek Week

The early Zionists were fond of the phrase "the rustle of history's wings." The inauguration of an agricultural cooperative in a Jewish village was brushed by the wings of history. A meeting between the secretary of a kibbutz and the mukhtar of a neighboring Arab village was always a historic milestone. The first Hebrew watermelon north of the ancient town of Sepphoris was clearly a historic watermelon.

The Hypnosis of the Past

This historical inflationism of the early Zionists was not a sign of spiritual self-effacement vis-à-vis the past. On the contrary. The first furrow after two thousand years betokened pride that

---

The name Amalek represents a Canaanite tribe that attacked the Israelites in the wilderness (Exodus 17:8–16). The Lord instructed the Israelites to wipe Amalek from their memory. Amalek has come to signify an archetypal enemy of the Jews.

the present could provide a fitting response to the past. The historic plow was historic in the eyes of the plowmen precisely because they viewed it as a symbol that the Jews, who had existed outside history for two thousand years, attempting to float above it, to flatten themselves beneath its feet, or to hide behind its back, had decided to reenter history, to become an active force within it, shaping and influencing it—no longer to be a passive, submissive victim. The Zionist credo, in a nutshell, was the aspiration "to become masters of our own fate."

Now it turns out that the major obstacle to our reentry into history is, ironically, our enslavement to the horrors of history. The addiction to memory has debilitated the addict. "History poisoning" is an obstacle to making history. Precisely the paralyzing intensity of the past is the most dangerous threat to the Zionist future. Zionism drew enormous motivating power from the historic past. But the past is also a stagnating force, stultifying and contradicting the very purpose of Zionism.

"The rustle of history's wings" thus expresses the drawn-out, covert struggle between two powerful impulses: the obsessive wish to relive the historical experience over and over again, and the desire to break out of the stocks of the past in order to try to shape the present and the future as free men.

On the one hand, Zionism had to relate unceasingly to the collective memory of the Jews in order to draw from it inspiration, justification, and ardor. On the other hand, Zionism had to destroy without mercy what the writer Yosef Haim Brenner called "the hypnosis of the past."

Spain, Germany, Russia, and Various Other Amaleks

These reflections have become particularly relevant in recent days. The president of Israel has paid a state visit to the land of Hitler. At the same time, Israel's foreign minister was in Spain, from which our ancestors were expelled and whose soil had been consistently ostracized by the Jews for five hundred years. From Spain, our foreign minister went straight to Rome, the city of Titus, destroyer of Jerusalem, to meet with official representatives of Russia, which persecuted Jews both before and after the 1917 revolution. All this was done with the aim of promoting an international peace conference under the auspices of "the evil Gentile world," in the hope that such a conference would further the peace process with "the inheritors of the seven biblical enemy nations of Canaan."

It is no wonder, then, that the air here has been thick these days with the rustle of history's wings, or, to be precise, with the rustle of wings of history hatred. It is no wonder that the guardians of the commandment to "Remember" have raised a clamor and tried to turn the week before Passover into "Amalek Week."

Indeed, for them every day of the year is Amalek Day, and Amalek lies beside them every night. Amalek is my rock; an Amalek in every pot. Amalek is a code word betraying a psychic urge to walk out on history and to view the world as ongoing theater, in which, again and again, everywhere and at all times, seventy Amalekian wolves, their fangs dripping, surround one snowy-white lamb. One lost sheep. One kid led to the slaughter. And there cannot be, nor will there be, any change in this scenario until the coming of the Messiah. Anyone who tries to change it is an enemy of Israel and a servant of Amalek.

Sackcloth and Ashes

The issue is not whether the president of the State of Israel should have paid an official visit to Germany and, if so, when and how, with or without traveling in a special Luftwaffe aircraft, with or without loud declarations about "the triumph of the six million." Nor is the issue the benefits or dangers of an international peace conference, the value of the visit to Spain, the balance sheet of the Soviet meeting, or the question of whether there is an Arab partner with whom to make peace, and at what price. These are weighty questions indeed, but they are all ephemeral in comparison with the fundamental question: Is Israel permitted to send its president to Germany or is it not? to shake hands with Spain? to talk to Russia? to make peace with its enemies? to become part of "Gentile" world history? Are we or are we not permitted to do things our ancestors never did? In other words: What is the weight of the past as opposed to the needs of the present and the future? Apart from the obligation to remember, is there also a right to forget? Are we allowed to try to shape history, or only to drape ourselves in it, like sackcloth and ashes, and to sit forever mourning for our dead? to sit behind barred doors and shuttered windows, telephone disconnected, our backs to the wicked world and our faces to the awful past, our backs to the living and our faces to the dead, to sit thus, day and night, and to remember what was done unto us by Amalek, until the coming of the Messiah—or until the second coming of Amalek?

The Theory of the Ghetto

Israel's president visits Germany, its foreign minister visits Spain, and Russia and Arabia and Rome are in the headlines.

123

Such headlines touch our primal experiences, those from our individual and collective nursery-school days. One could almost speak of a Jewish identity composed of the collection of injustices inflicted on us by our enemies over thousands of years. Virtually every one of our holidays reminds us of "what was done unto you by Amalek": Rome, Spain, Russia, Arabia, Greece, Germany, Babylonia, Egypt, England, and all the others.

Behind the invective of the past week, behind the hysterical accusations of betrayal and sellout of national honor, the hypnosis of the past flickered once more. And, as usual, it was the voices of those who define themselves as "ultra-Zionists," preaching to us about our Zionist flabbiness, who ironically betrayed their fear of the outside world, their hatred of all Gentiles, their anti-Zionist urge to break off all contact with the world and lock ourselves, once and for all, in the museum of our calamities, among the ghosts of our martyrs, in the cellar of the humiliation and insult we have suffered. Only in that cellar, in the suffocating ritual incense for the dead, in a brackish cloud of grudges, self-righteousness, and self-pity, only there do they feel truly safe and warm.

Thus some professional Jewish hard-liners offer us an Israel, not as a home for Israelis, but as one big museum of martyrdom, populated, not by citizens, but by a perpetual assembly of prayer, of perpetual mourners commemorating the perpetual Amalekian pogrom.

Hiding behind all this is great misery. And also the urge to flee from history—which compels us to make constant choices between various shades of gray—and to retreat into a simple, comfortable world divided, without nuances, into a handful of children of light, on one side, and hordes of children of darkness, rising up in every generation to destroy us and be done with us, on the other. Pure and simple. To disengage ourselves from history, to return to the ghettos, to wait for the next pogrom. To escape from Zionism into the hypnosis of the past. To abandon the chance to mold history, and, instead, to return to our old habit of lying down and flattening ourselves under its wheels.

Buzzard or Dove

Beyond the legitimate argument over the appropriateness of the president's trip to Germany, over the purpose of the visit to Spain, over the effectiveness of an international peace conference or the price of peace, we can sense the fateful debate over the rustle of history's wings: Is the rustle of wings that of an eternal buzzard swooping down, time and again, on the carcasses of every generation—the same buzzard, the same carcasses, ever since the exodus from Egypt and down to this very day? Or may we sometimes send out a dove to see whether the waters have receded?

In political terms: Are we to behave like a nation-state, or act like a ghetto? to be Zionists or ultra-Orthodox? None of this is new, of course. What is new, perhaps, is only the carnival tendency of the anti-Zionist camp to disguise itself in an ultra-Zionist mask, to hide its traumas behind arrogant nationalist slogans.

Davar, April 13, 1987

The Rift Is an Accomplished Fact

Rabbi Menachem Fruman asked me to reply to an article, published in *Davar,* in which he called for a dialogue between Gush Emunim and the Labor movement. This came at a time when the leaders of Gush Emunim were involved in a struggle to obtain a pardon for the members of the Jewish terrorist organization, whom they described as "good patriots who erred a bit."

I have always been a strong opponent of Gush Emunim, but, nevertheless, in the fall of 1982 I went to speak with some of its people at their homes in Tekoa and Ofra, in the West Bank. I did not go in order to "convert" them or to "reconcile" with them, but, rather, to study at firsthand the nature of the group. And maybe I managed to learn a thing or two about them. When they asked me to address them, I concentrated mostly on an attempt to make clear to my listeners that their opponents also have unbreachable tenets and that any attempt on their part to trample our basic humanist principles will be regarded as a declaration of war on us, and a fathomless rift will ensue. It came to light a year later that among my listeners in Ofra there had been several of the Jewish terrorists, including one of the leaders of those who, we now know, had been plotting to blow up Arab buses, together with their passengers, in Jerusalem and to bomb the mosques on the Temple Mount. They apparently assumed that I and my kind are "softies," and concluded that I was talking about the danger of a rift just to amuse myself; that if they committed a despicable massacre, then, at most, I'd sit down with them the day after the slaughter, at some symposium, and we'd discuss our differences over a cup of tea. Or maybe they took into account the possibility of a rift and decided to let me and all those like me go to hell. Or else they really didn't understand the meaning of the word "rift," and thought I meant a difference of opinion in some panel discussion.

However, a rift is what we have. It exists not only and not even primarily because of the Jewish terrorist murderers and their accomplices, but primarily because of their defenders and the nature of the defense that most of Gush Emunim has built up for them. I wish to emphasize that Gush Emunim is *not* a terrorist organization, and almost all its people are *not* murderers. The issue is the type of arguments they enlist in seeking a pardon for the murderers.

Correction: If Gush Emunim were to seek a pardon for murderers, it would not be so bad. Even a murderer, under extenuating circumstances, may be deserving of our compassion.

But the "Gush" is in no way asking for a pardon for murderers. What it seeks is a pardon, if not legal redress, if not, indeed, hero's medals, for "those boys who took the law into their own hands a little." They do not believe that taking the law into one's own hands is a serious violation of religious law, but consider it at most a "flaw resulting from rashness." I will no longer talk with Gush Emunim, at least not until Gush Emunim stands up and states that it is seeking this pardon for *murderers*, not for "mischief-makers." When it stands up and declares that it wants a pardon for murderers, I will talk with its spokesmen. Until then, there will be a chasm between me and all the defenders of those who take the law into their own hands. Until then, there is a rift. (Let me not generalize:

127

Rabbi Yoel Bin-Nun and you, Rabbi Fruman, and several others have called murder "murder." With you, I'll talk. Although I will talk harshly about the correlation between the lasting occupation and the loss of one's humanity.)

After reading your article, I fear you have not understood the depth of this rift. You seem to think that it is business as usual. "Thou shalt not murder" has all-encompassing validity, contrary to what my would-be partners in dialogue from Gush Emunim contend: "De jure—thou shalt not murder; de facto—thou shalt not murder a Jew." Until Gush Emunim, as a movement, stands up and publicly states that the blood of a Jewish child killed by Arab terrorists is no redder than the blood of the Arab child A'isha Al-Bahsh killed in Nablus by a member of Gush Emunim named Yossi Har-Noy, and until Gush Emunim declares that the murder of yeshiva students is no different from the murder of students at the Islamic College—until then, I have nothing to say to Gush Emunim, apart from those individuals who agree—publicly—that it is forbidden to differentiate between one murder and another according to the identity of the murderer.

Davar, December 6, 1987

MARY KAFKA'S SUITCASE

(Written after viewing Claude Lanzmann's film Shoah)

Between Man
and Fellow Man

Claude Lanzmann's film *Shoah: An Oral History of the Ho-locaust* (1985) is the most powerful film I have ever seen. It is a creation that transforms the viewer.

After collapsing on the witness stand during the Eichmann trial, author Ka-Tzetnik said that Auschwitz was a "planet of ashes," that the destruction of the Jews took place "on a different planet," and that whoever had not been there would never understand. With this, he concisely expressed the same idea that teachers, public figures, and orators have tried to instill in us in their efforts to "inculcate an awareness of the Holocaust in native-born Israelis." Something inhuman happened there; satanic, metaphysic. As though history had been broken in the middle and transplanted to another planet. The Holocaust, so they told us, and we repeated it to ourselves, is "incomprehensible."

The very term "Holocaust" creates an extrahuman ap-

The quotations from *Shoah* in this section are based on the author's recollection; they were not taken verbatim from the film.

131

proach to destruction. A holocaust is an outburst of natural forces, which humans neither cause nor have the power to prevent or to influence, nor even to understand its causes and the manner of its occurrence. Earthquake, flood, tornado.

Claude Lanzmann produced his film from a completely opposite position. His choice of the Hebrew title *Shoah* notwithstanding, we can, he offers, comprehend the destruction, not outside history, but within it, not beyond human nature, but as part of it, provided that we get down to the smallest details. None of this took place on another planet; it all happened on this earth, amid forests and meadows and peaceful hills, near idyllic villages, on the banks of rushing brooks, not far from people herding cows, playing cards, and fixing roofs in preparation for winter. There is no planet of ashes. The murdered victims were not saints. They were men, women, and children like anyone else—optimistic, frightened, and with limited imagination. The Polish peasants who happened to see the mass murders at close hand, indifferent witnesses, conniving witnesses, spiteful witnesses—they, too, were people like any others. And the survivors who appear in the film, who survived by cunning or by luck or by courage, were like any other human beings.

And, in truth, so were the murderers. They were not hairy devils, glowering beasts, or foaming fanatics, but men like all other men. Perhaps a little more stupid than the normal, average human, but not much more.

Not one figure, in nine and a half hours of Lanzmann, is larger than life.

Lanzmann's view is not to be confused with Hannah Arendt's well-known ingenious theory, in her book *Eichmann in Jerusalem*, of the "banality of evil." Lanzmann does not portray evil as a banal thing, but as something that masquerades as banal, a mixture of selfishness, stupidity, indifference, and ignorance, of prejudice tinged with malice. Lanzmann does not view the destruction of the Jews as a mythological drama or as a metaphysical cataclysm, nor as a theological experience or as an existential symbol. As if obsessed, he stubbornly re-creates, through minute technical details, the aggregate acts committed by human beings with the help of other human beings and in the presence of additional human beings to still other masses of human beings, almost all of whom did not comprehend, until their last moments, what was about to be done to them; who, when ordered to lend a hand in the undertaking, obeyed. Because it was not possible to disobey.

Even the handful of heroes in the uprising, even one or two speakers who understood what was happening, are not larger than life. There is no place in this movie for God, for the devil, for the spirit of history. The film distances the viewer from the widely held conception that maintains that the killing was the logical outgrowth of the "Germanic spirit," as well as from the common conclusion that "the germ lurks everywhere, and no individual and no people is immune."

One can find in the film moments of astonishing and penetrating exposure of the intensity of popular Christian anti-Semitism. But the Nazis who were interviewed made no use of Christian anti-Semitic clichés. They do not talk like anti-Semites at all. We had a dirty job to do, they say, and we did our duty under particularly difficult and ugly conditions.

There are almost no images, symbols, or cinematic metaphors in the film. There are a lot of trains that symbolize trains. The snow stands for snow, and the forests for forests. Perhaps Lanzmann is wary of metaphors because he knows that the murder of the Jews was the "literal" embodiment of an ancient metaphor.

What, then, is the focus of the film? It focuses primarily on a kind of "systems analysis," in the industrial sense of the term. The mass killings began in 1941 and were conducted by simple, clumsy methods: shootings and mass burials. Within a few months, in an effort to overcome "production constraints," trucks were employed to asphyxiate human beings with carbon monoxide fed in from the exhaust pipe, and the mass graves, which created problems, were replaced by open cremation pits. Within a year, more sophisticated killing methods were developed: Zyklon B gas chambers disguised as delousing showers, and crematoria capable of processing thousands of bodies each day. The process of perfecting the production line continued almost until Germany's surrender. The Holocaust boils down to just a handful of production engineers, laborious, inventive, and devoted to their task. And a handful of German executives at each of the murder sites. And several dozens of Ukrainian and Lithuanian "security guards," whose job it was to substitute for German manpower needed at the front. Thousands of Jewish "production workers," forced to attain a high level of efficiency and specialization. And, of course, a Polish population to provide the industry of death with an optimal "ecological" environment to implement the process.

None of this is "incomprehensible": Lanzmann chooses not to deal with "the birth of the horror from the spirit of Germanity"—the *Nibelungenlied*, Martin Luther, Goethe, Hegel, Chamberlain and Gobineau, Nietzsche and Richard Wagner—rather, he prefers to focus on the facts, on the technique; on how the survivors, murderers, and witnesses use words. Hitler himself, for example, "appears" only once: a Jewish artisan from Corfu, with a sheepish smile, demonstrates in front of the camera how to draw four pigs and then fold the paper in a certain way to make a portrait of the Führer. Nothing more. There is no Satan. The murder of the Jews appears here as an intrahuman affair. I almost wrote "as a matter between man and his fellow man."

> *Here in this transport*
> *I, Eve*
> *With my son Abel*
> *If you see my older son*
> *Cain, son of Adam,*
> *Tell him that I am*
>> —DAN PAGIS, "Written in Pencil
>> in the Sealed Wagon," from
>> the collection *Metamorphosis*

Tell him that I am what?

Nothing. Silence. That is how Lanzmann's film, too, concludes. A sealed train moving along the tracks. And silence. No lesson, no moral.

Except, perhaps, for one trivial conclusion: All those involved—Jews, Germans, Poles—have fingers; they all have ears, lips, and eyelashes. They all have grown old. They all get dressed, eat, sit, wake up, and go to sleep. Some of them are suffering from illnesses and infirmities; others look fine for their advanced age. Nothing has come to a conclusion or a resolution, except for the lives of the millions murdered. The Holocaust is still going on because the suffering continues. And the forgetting continues, including the forgetting by dint of a stern decision to forget. Everything flows. It is both possible and impossible, according to Lanzmann, to take a dip in the same river twice. It is both possible and impossible to sit in Cain's living room, over a cup of tea, and chat with him about Eve and Abel, who were in the sealed wagon.

"How did you feel?" Lanzmann asks Franz Suchomel, an SS man, old and ailing, in front of a hidden camera. "How did you feel when you first saw the bodies spilling out of the gas chamber at Treblinka?"

"People fell out like potatoes," the aging murderer recalls in a tone of wonder and sadness. "Naturally," he adds, "we . . . cried like old women at first. It was . . . catastrophic, Herr Lanzmann. Do you understand? Catastrophic."

Strong Nerves of Divinity and True German Irony

For forty years now we have been teaching ourselves that the murder of European Jewry can be explained but not understood. It was pronounced incomprehensible because, "if you were not there yourself, you are incapable of . . ." and so forth. Yet it could be explained because there is "context" and "meaning." And so explanations piled upon explanations: from Jean-Paul Sartre to Friedlander, from Hannah Arendt to Viktor Frankl, from Elie Wiesel to Menachem Begin. It has been explained from a Marxist perspective and in a theological context. The intellectual significance and the political background have been explored. And it has been explained in terms of historiosophy and by psychoanalytical methods, among others.

Claude Lanzmann tells us the exact opposite: There is no point in explaining, but, for once, let us try to comprehend.

Comprehension is possible, provided we are willing to immerse ourselves in the most minute detail. What time was it? Where did they put their clothes and shoes? How cold was it? What color were the death trucks? How many minutes did it take to get from the platform to the crematorium? Who paid for the transports? How did they load and unload? What exactly did they do with the thighbones that were too heavy to be burned in the regular way?

This microscopic detail is what gives Lanzmann's creation a Tolstoyan, Joycean, Proustian dimension. The film *Shoah* resembles *War and Peace*, and in another sense it resembles *Ulysses* and *Remembrance of Things Past*. It is a journey into memory that aspires, ideally, to document everything: each fraction of a second multiplied by four years, multiplied by six million. As we said: an obsession with detail. Ideally, this is a film without an end; a film seeking to have the screening time of one thousand years and more. We are told that Lanzmann shot 350 hours of film, of which he has shown us less than ten. As a matter of principle, this film ought to continue until the end of time.

> *I am man, but You are God, You have a*
>   *Creator's imagination.*
> *Surely You were there among Your flocks*
> *In Auschwitz and Majdanek,*
> *In Belżec and Treblinka,*
> *In Ponari and Bergen-Belsen—*
> *You know how to describe that spectacle in its*
>   *every line, every groan, every glance.*
> *You have the imagination, and You have the strong*
>   *nerves of divinity—*
>
> —URI ZVI GREENBERG,
> "Streets of the River"

We don't have the "strong nerves of divinity." We won't watch a continuous showing of, let us say, six hours each day over a period of fifty years. Lanzmann's attempt is therefore doomed to failure in the same sense that the efforts of Tolstoy,

Joyce, and Proust were shattered by the limits of human time. It is not possible to document everything. It is impossible to describe that spectacle in its every line, every groan, every glance. But that is the thrust of Lanzmann's efforts. It is his way of comprehending the "incomprehensible."

If Adolf Hitler had given strict orders to destroy all the house pets and farm animals throughout the Third Reich, dogs and cats, parrots and goldfish, horses, cows, goats, sheep, and pigs, we can assume there would have been outbreaks of civil disobedience throughout occupied Europe and in Germany itself. After all, one cares for one's dog or cat. People would have tried to hide their house pets until the mad verdict was over. The extermination of horses, cows, and pigs would have incensed millions whose livelihood this would have jeopardized, not to mention the threat to the war effort, or the fact that everyone would have realized immediately that whoever had given the orders to destroy the animals was stark raving mad.

But there is no point in such reflections: a Jew is neither a goldfish nor a pig. In the Department of Jewish Affairs of the Reich Ministry of Defense, at 116 Kurfürstendamm in Berlin, Adolf Eichmann and his aides sat and organized the killing of six million human beings in accordance with vague, sketchy instructions in a letter ("to carry out all preparations with regard to . . . a total solution of the Jewish question") that had been sent from the office of Hermann Göring to Reinhard Heydrich. The enormous project was carried out without burdening the German taxpayer with a single penny's expenditure: historian Raul Hilberg explains on camera that the Gestapo purchased group-fare tickets at a discount (half-price for children) from the Reich railroad authority. The tickets were paid for with Jewish money expropriated by the Gestapo from bank accounts owned by Jews. The special tracks, the camps and barracks, the disrobing rooms, the gas chambers, and the crematoria were built by Jewish slave labor. The production line itself was operated by a handful of Germans, aided by Lithuanian and Ukrainian guard units. The "job" was done almost entirely by Jewish "task forces." And from Paris to Bialystok, from Amsterdam to Salonika, Christian Europe stood by and watched the disappearance of the Jews—and kept silent.

Some of the Polish peasants in Lanzmann's film explain the silence better than all the philosophers and their theories. They, the Jews, always knew it would come, that this was bound to happen to them someday. And we, the peasants, knew it was bound to come. And in their hearts, they, the Jews, knew that they had it coming to them. And we, the peasants, also knew they had it coming to them, because they were all rich, and very, very dishonest, and they always had a bad smell about them, and they weren't even Polish, but held all of Poland in their hands, and they had exploited Poland and handed Jesus Christ over for crucifixion, and even agreed, in front of Pontius Pilate, that his blood would be on their heads and on the heads of their children. So why the wonder that it finally happened? The Jews weren't all that surprised and neither were we. Even so, it's a bit of a shame about them. Even Jesus didn't want to take vengeance this far. It would have been much better if they'd all gone to Palestine and been done with it.

Paradoxically, horrifyingly, this last sentence is a kind of Zionist consensus on the whole film: It would have been better if they had all gone to Palestine and been done with it.

It seems that this sentence would have been endorsed by all those interviewed: the survivors, the Polish peasants of Chelmno, the Nazi murderers in the film; indeed, almost all the characters, perhaps even Claude Lanzmann himself.

But Lanzmann lives in Paris, and most of the Jews he interviewed are scattered all over, from Switzerland to New York.

First scene: Simon Srebnik, the "Chelmno nightingale," returns to the place of the mass killing forty years later. A Polish peasant rows him in a boat down a lovely little river, and Simon sits there and sings. He survived mostly because of his melodious voice. At the age of thirteen, after the Lodz ghetto, after the death of his parents, he was brought to the camp to serve the overlords with his toil and his songs. This Simon must have been an extraordinarily sweet child: even the aged Polish residents of Chelmno and the wife of the local Nazi German schoolmaster clearly remember the charm of his Polish and German singing. And they unanimously say how happy they are that this lovely child was saved from death. The Gestapo apparently treated him like a talisman or mascot of their unit: His legs were put in iron chains, and he learned to hop with his legs tied and to sing for them the sentimental kitsch songs from the regions of their birth, thus soothing their nostalgia and easing the pangs of their homesickness.

"It was always this peaceful here," Simon says. "Always. When they burned two thousand people—Jews—every day it was just as peaceful." The flames, he recalls, reached "zum Himmel" (to the sky); yet, everything was quiet. Nobody ever raised his voice around here.

Lanzmann, a relentless interviewer, asks Simon Srebnik to sing one of those songs. And Simon sings amid the Polish landscape. His tenor voice is still very pleasant, and the peasants stop to listen. These peasants live in houses that once belonged to Jews.

Now silence reigns all over this land of death
And brightness and light and the song of birds and many
  colors.
Strings of small towns along rivers and woods.
The cities in the plain exalt the cross . . .
Ivan and Stepan are dwelling in our homes there—
                              —URI ZVI GREENBERG,
                          "Streets of the River"

Mordechai Podchlebnik is the second survivor of Chelmno. "It's not good for me to talk about this," he says with a smile. Lanzmann, as usual, presses for details: numbers, locations, methods, facts. How did they kill? Where did they do the killing? How did they dispose of the bodies? And Podchlebnik, although "it's not good for me to talk about this," begins to describe everything, in detail, without losing his smile. "Ask him," Lanzmann says to the interpreter, "why he smiles all the time." And the man, like a Jew from a story by Sholom Aleichem, still smiling, answers the question with another question: "So what does he want me to do? Cry?" And, after a moment of reflection, he adds, "And if you're alive, it's better to smile."

Motke Zaidl did not go to Poland with Lanzmann. He is interviewed in a forest in Israel, not in the woods of Ponari. (The place resembles Ponari, he says, except that there were no stones in Ponari. Also, the Lithuanian woods are much, much denser than this forest in Israel.)

"How did you react the first time you unloaded corpses, when the gas van doors were opened?" Lanzmann asks.

"What could I do? The third day, I put my wife and children in the pit and asked to be killed also. But the Germans

142

said I was strong enough to work, that I wouldn't be killed yet."

Lanzmann: "Was the weather very cold?"

Zaidl: "It was very cold—in the winter of 1942, early January."

We hear this question and the answer many times throughout the film. Even an SS man agrees without hesitation: "Yes, sir, we were very cold. The poor Jews, who were completely naked, might just have been even colder. But maybe they warmed themselves in the railroad cars, during the ride, because it was very crowded in there and that created a little body heat. It's hard to tell."

In Vilnius (Vilna), in the Ponari woods, they didn't burn the bodies at first, but buried them in mass graves. And that was no good. On this point, too, one of the Nazis interviewed agrees: The graves were shallow, so the soil expanded and cracked from the gases emitted by the swelling corpses, creating a terrible stench. "Schrecklich, sehr schrecklich." "It was awful," and there was a danger of epidemics. Another way had to be found.

"They buried them," says Yitzhak Dugin, formerly of Vilna, "like sardines in a can. They put all the Jews of Vilna and its vicinity into the soil at Ponari. Ninety thousand altogether. But on January 1, 1944, we got an order from the Gestapo commander of Vilna to open up all the ditches; to take the bodies out and burn them so that no trace would remain. They gave us a plan: to start from the beginning—to start by opening the oldest ditches. When we got to the last ditch, the bodies there were still fresh and in very good condition, because of the cold. When the last mass grave was opened, I dug up my whole family. My mother and my sisters. Three sisters and their children. They had been in the earth only four months, and they hadn't rotted because of the cold.

I recognized them by their faces and by their clothes. Twenty-four thousand people were buried in that ditch. The deeper you dug, the more you saw bodies pressed together flat like boards. You'd take a body and it would crumble completely right away. At first they wouldn't let us use tools. They told us: Get used to doing it all with your hands. If we cried, they'd beat us mercilessly with sticks. They also didn't let us use the words 'bodies' or 'victims.' They forced us to use the words 'Figuren' or 'Dreck' or 'Shmattes.' If you said 'victims,' you got a beating. We had to burn these Figuren so that no trace was left of them."

In the woods around the Sobibor death camp, too, they tried to cover their tracks, to obliterate every trace. A Polish witness says that in Treblinka, after the camp was closed in 1943, the Germans went to the trouble of planting pine trees, "five-year-old saplings they were," so that by 1944 you could no longer see any sign of what happened there.

Lanzmann hasn't found anyone to ask about the reason for this German discretion: Was it fear of punishment in case Germany lost the war? If so, then punishment by whom? Was it shame, perhaps? But if so, then shame before whom?

At the time of the Eichmann trial in Jerusalem, the West German newspaper *Nüremberger Nachrichten* published, on April 26, 1961, the following statement:

"In light of the preconceived notions that, partly due to insufficient information, partly due to lack of understanding, and partly due to simple malice, have accumulated in the minds of certain people, especially abroad, concerning National Socialism and especially its racial policy, we have assumed that the Eichmann trial would increase this lack of understanding. But now it appears that, together with a great deal of negativism—the trial has brought to light facts that may offset the incorrect evaluations that prevailed before—he [Eichmann] was a decent young man . . . who, by his own testimony, always merely carried out the abominable tasks that were demanded of him. He did so unwillingly and with inner resistance. . . . He confessed that he could not consider becoming a doctor, for example, because even an open cut made him sick to his stomach and he couldn't look. . . . In the Chelmno camp Eichmann once watched a group of naked Jews being executed by the gas engine, and he had to turn away. . . . Indeed the cries of the victims grated on his nerves. . . ."

Another excerpt, from a different sort of German newspaper, *Die Deutsche Zeitung*, of May 25, 1961, said:

". . . One of the witnesses, testifying about the methods of annihilation in Galicia, was asked why, in light of the expected annihilation, the inmates of the ghetto did not gather their strength for one last counterattack, even if it was hopeless. What a lack of understanding! What an academic question! . . . No one who has not been through all this can truly understand. . . . The arguments of the witness, I say [the speaker is the German reporter who covered the Eichmann trial], surely hold good for the German people as well: No one who did not go through what the Germans went through can understand. The war, which they perceived as a battle for survival forced upon them from the outside, the day-to-day worries about self-preservation, fear of the system . . ."

And at the end of his article this reporter adds some words of admiration for the beauty of the people of Israel: "A young nation that bears arms with enthusiasm, that loves its homeland without intellectual doubts, that truly identifies its nationalism with its personality. Come, they say, and look at us: Do we look like Jews . . . ? Their faces bear no resemblance to the traditional features . . . of the diaspora Jew."

(Both excerpts were taken from an anthology, *The Eichmann Trial in West German Public Opinion,* in Hebrew, edited by Avraham Bartura.)

A Polish man in Lanzmann's film, maybe from the city of Kolo or from Chelmno, describes the reception given to the Jewish deportees on one of the railroad platforms. "It was . . . true German irony."

They Were Definitely Created in God's Image

Here's an example of "true German irony": Rudolf Vrba, well spoken, charismatic, elegant in a well-tailored suit, who escaped from Auschwitz on April 7, 1944, describes, with a slight, sardonic smile, his work as a registration clerk at a death camp:

"It was night at Auschwitz. They woke us for work. On the platform, at ten-yard intervals, stood the SS troops with dogs and submachine guns. The platform was flooded with blinding spotlights. We waited. The locomotive pulled in slowly. The train came to a stop. One of the Unterscharführers moved from one car to the next and unlocked them from the outside. People peered out of the windows, which were covered with barbed wire. They had been en route for ten or fifteen days. They were hungry, thirsty, and exhausted. Inside the cars, the living sat on the bodies of the dead and the dying. They had no idea what this station was. The name Auschwitz told them nothing. They streamed out of the cars, and the Germans shouted, "Raus! Schnell!" and hit them with whips and sticks.

"But at one point, one of the German officers spoke to the crowd on the platform with unusual courtesy: 'Welcome,' he said. 'We apologize for the inconvenient travel conditions. In a little while each of you will get a cup of tea and you'll be well taken care of. You'll be just fine here.' "

In a secret address delivered to SS generals in Poznań on October 4, 1943, Gestapo chief Heinrich Himmler praised his unsung heroes, who carried out their difficult, thankless task:

". . . I also want to talk to you quite frankly on a very grave matter. Among ourselves it should be mentioned quite frankly, and yet we will never speak of it publicly. I mean . . . the extermination of the Jewish race. . . . Most of *you* must know what it means when 100 corpses are lying side by side, or 500, or 1,000. To have stuck it out and at the same time—apart from exceptions caused by human weakness—to have remained decent fellows, that is what has made us hard. This is a page of glory in our history which has never been written and is never to be written. . . ."

"On August 31, [1942,] Himmler had ordered an *Einsatz* detachment to execute a hundred inmates of the Minsk prison, so that he could see how it was done. According to Bach-Zalewski, a high officer in the SS who was present, Himmler almost swooned when he saw the effect of the first volley from the firing squad. A few minutes later, when the shots failed to kill two Jewish women outright, the SS Führer became hysterical. One result of this experience was an order from Himmler that henceforth the women and children should not be shot but dispatched in the gas vans." (Both quotes from William Shirer, *The Rise and Fall of the Third Reich*.)

·

Next, the camera zeroes in on a mountain of suitcases at the museum in Auschwitz. Each suitcase bears the name of its owner, his address, and in some instances the date of his birth. The first suitcase we see belonged to one Mary Kafka. The last one was that of Herman Pasternak.

The Poles: a slim locomotive driver who, fortified by special vodka rations from the Germans, once drove the deportation trains of Jews to the Treblinka death camp, now once again drives a train to the Treblinka station. Upon reaching the station sign he stops, twists his body partway out of the driver's cab, and turns to the Jews who are no longer there. His face resembles that of an old fox; he moves his hand across his throat in a slow gesture of slaughter. All the survivors remember that, at each stop, Polish villagers made the same gesture across their throats at the sight of the packed trains. "We only wanted to warn them," the Polish witnesses explain. But the gesture expresses malice and sadism.

"We went on working as usual in the fields nearby," Czeslaw Borowy, a fat, merry peasant, recalls, and the neighboring farmers confirm his story: "Sometimes we'd hear terrible screams."

"Wasn't it hard for you to work, hearing these terrible screams?" Claude Lanzmann asks.

"You get used to it. You can get used to anything."

There were sixty to eighty cars in each transport, Borowy adds. The fat rich Jews from abroad arrived in fancy sleepers. Our Jews, the Polish ones, he says, came hungry and thirsty. They waited inside the cars. They cried and begged for water. Some of them were naked. "Sometimes we gave them a little water to drink. Us. The Poles. It was very dangerous. You could have got killed for doing it."

"Was it cold?"

"It was very cold. Fifteen, twenty degrees below zero."

The train driver with the foxlike features stands pensively in the Treblinka station.

"Why are you sad?" asks Lanzmann.

"Because they killed a lot of people. Now I don't understand anymore how one human being could do this to another human being."

Lanzmann interviews Abraham Bomba, a barber now living in Holon, on a boat near the seashore, with the luxury hotels of Tel Aviv in the background against a dazzling blue sky. "The Jews always dreamed," he says. "They always had this dream that one day the Messiah would come and take them to freedom. Even there, in the ghetto, they dreamed about it. I was in the second transport from Częstochowa. I understood right away that this was no good. They're telling us that they're taking us to work, but what kind of work is that, when they're taking old women and babies with us? But there was no choice. A man has to dream. Or to hope. Without that, you can't live. So we believed them anyway."

SS officer Franz Suchomel was not only photographed by a hidden camera, but also recorded, by means of a car with sophisticated listening equipment parked near his house. Lanzmann gave Suchomel a promise, which he did not intend to keep, to protect his anonymity, and he did not bother—rightly—to delete his promise from his film.

"How are you today, Herr Suchomel? How is your heart?"

"Today the weather's actually excellent for me. The barometric pressure is comfortable."

"If you get too emotional, if you don't feel well, give me a sign like this with your hand and we'll take a break."

There is no need for a break: Herr Suchomel does not get too emotional and he feels fine throughout the interview.

"Thank you very much. Everything is fine. When did we arrive at Treblinka? On the eighteenth of August? No? Perhaps the twenty-fourth? Ja. Ja. Correct. About the twentieth. They were working full blast to empty out the Warsaw ghetto. They also brought trains full of Jews from France. No. No. That's an exaggeration, there were never more than three trains a day, with three thousand Jews in each one. Approximately. A great many died during the trip; they were crowded, and the others were half dead also. The gas chambers were too small and couldn't keep up with the job. The Jews had to wait. It was hard for them, and also for us. And in the meantime, some of them had guessed what was going to happen to them. Perhaps they heard the motor of the tank whose exhaust piped gas into the chamber, and figured it out. That was before they improved it and switched to Zyklon gas."

"Herr Suchomel, before you arrived there, did you know what Treblinka was?"

"Ach, nein! Ach, nein! I didn't know. I didn't want to go there. They told me, 'You will just guard the tailors and shoemakers to make sure they do their work properly.' That was the Führer's order, to resettle them. Just as we arrived, they opened the gas chambers and people spilled out like potatoes. Dreadful! Dreadful! Especially the smell was terrible. It smelled for ki-lo-meters! Eberele, the camp commandant, telephoned Lublin and said, 'I can't go on like this. We have to take a break. I can't keep up.' Within a day the top commandant, [SS Major Christian] Wirth, arrived. Wirth had much more experience—he had been commandant at Belżec before. He saw what was going on—that horror—and he im-

151

mediately gave orders to stop the transports so they could catch up with the work.

"The bodies were piled up—like that—and we couldn't get rid of them. There was maybe three feet of blood and excrement. Nobody was willing to clean up the filth. Even the Jews preferred to be shot. They felt bad about having to bury their people like that. Finally they brought some kind of long belts and cleaned up the filth. The Jews did it together with the SS. Those were orders. In this instance, the SS men gave a hand, too.

"Treblinka," Suchomel says modestly, "was just a primitive production line, but it was efficient. Remember what I said: primitive but efficient. You can't compare it to Auschwitz. Auschwitz was a factory. But Treblinka also worked well."

The "dirty work" was done by Jews. Filip Müller, a Czech Jew, a member of the Sonderkommando who survived five "selections" in Auschwitz, describes how a "production failure" could hold up the whole process for some time: In one instance, inexperienced workers allowed the ventilation pump of the crematoria to get overheated, and it was necessary to revert to improvised burial in the ground for a while. "Every malfunction could have saved many people. But there were not many malfunctions. They taught us to work very quickly and expertly."

The historian Raul Hilberg says in the film that the Germans made very few innovations. They did invent the gas chambers. That was something new. But almost all the rest was copied from historical precedents: the exclusion of Jews from certain jobs, the ban on intermarriage, the ban on Christian women under the age of forty-five working in Jewish households, the yellow patch with the Star of David, the isolation of the Jews in ghettos. All these had been tried before, by religious and secular authorities during the nearly two thousand years of Christianity. There was a large pool of accumulated knowledge, which the Nazis merely applied with precision and on a large scale. Most of the laws and regulations enacted by the Third Reich, at least until 1939, but even after that, were not original. The image of the Jew in Nazi propaganda was copied from the image of the Jew at the time of Martin Luther. The Nazis became original and creative only at the stage of the "final solution." Here they had to invent, because they had no appropriate precedents.

Since the fourth century, continues Hilberg, Jew-hatred has progressed in stages: 1. You are forbidden to live in our midst as Jews (result: ghettos). 2. You are forbidden to live among us (result: expulsion). 3. You are forbidden to live altogether (result: total annihilation).

Stage 3 represented the Nazi innovation. The bureaucracy was given only the most generalized directive and was forced to use imagination and originality to deal with the problems: How to organize? How to deceive? How to transport? How to expropriate property? How to finance? How to kill? How to get rid of the bodies?

The Nazi solutions were technical, "gray." But hidden behind the grayness was a brilliant grand scheme: to transport millions of people to their death in the shortest, simplest way possible, by means of a formula based on a carefully calculated and measured dose of deceit, intimidation, and cunning, and on breaking the willpower of the victims so that they would not believe what awaited them and would not be moved to such desperate acts as escape, resistance, or bursts of mass panic. Any display of panic was liable to hinder the process. Therefore, euphemisms had to be used, even in internal documents; explicit expressions had to be censored; innocent, encouraging words, such as "resettlement," "job training," "special treatment," "merchandise" had to be chosen. The killing itself was described by classic anti-Semitic metaphors: Cleansing the world of Jews; cleansing the body of parasites; cleansing the Jews of their diseases. (This last metaphor also became widely current among the Jews themselves; Zionists made much use of it.) And so the Jews were taken to be washed, to the shower that would cleanse them so that they might "turn over a new leaf." Deep in their hearts, the Jews, too, wanted to be cleansed and to turn over a new leaf. The shower metaphor is thus illumined by sparks of genius, far from the bureaucratic grayness usually attributed to the Nazis. The imagination of the murderers fed on the limited imagination of the murdered. The creative imagination of Hitler, Himmler, Eichmann, and Golovenchik surpassed the imagination of Mary Kafka and Herman Pasternak. The only remains of Kafka and Pasternak were empty suitcases in a heap of baggage.

In *Eichmann in Jerusalem*, Hannah Arendt argues that evil is not satanic and that we should not attribute to it a lofty, shadowy dimension, a romantic-demonic mysterious magic. In her words, evil is "banal." The Nazi crime had been committed by petty bureaucrats. The killers could have been Everyman, and only technological "mass society" and its impersonal concepts made the achievement of the "final solution" possible. In 1938, Thomas Mann expressed somewhat similar thoughts in an essay with the astonishing title "Brother Hitler." Mann never repeated these words after the outbreak of World War II.

In Saul Bellow's *Mr. Sammler's Planet*, there is the following conversation:

" 'The idea being,' said Margotte, 'that here is no great spirit of evil. Those people were too insignificant, Uncle. They were just ordinary lower-class people, administrators, small bureaucrats. . . . A mass society does not produce great criminals. . . . It's like instead of a forest with enormous trees, you have to think of small plants with shallow roots.' "

Arkin says, "Enough, enough of this Weimar *schmaltz.* Cut it, Margotte!"

And Uncle Sammler, that Cyclops saved from the killing, says: "The idea of making the century's great crime look dull is not banal. Politically, psychologically, the Germans had an idea of genius. The banality was only camouflage. What better way to get the curse out of murder than to make it look ordinary, boring, or trite? With horrible political insight they found a way to disguise the thing. Intellectuals do not understand. They get their notions about matters like this from literature. They expect a wicked hero like Richard III. But do you think the Nazis didn't know what murder was? Everybody (except certain bluestockings) knows what murder is. That is very old human knowledge. The best and purest human beings, from the beginning of time, have understood that life is sacred. To defy that old understanding is not banality. There was a conspiracy against the sacredness of life. Banality is the adopted disguise of a very powerful will to abolish conscience. Is such a project trivial? Only if human life is trivial. This woman professor's [Hannah Arendt] enemy is modern civilization itself. She is only using the Germans to attack the twentieth century. . . . Making use of a tragic history to promote the foolish ideas of Weimar intellectuals."

> No, no: they were definitely
> Human beings: uniforms, boots.

How shall I explain? They were created in God's image.
I was a shadow.
I had a different Creator.
            —DAN PAGIS, "Slavery,"
                from the collection *Metamorphosis*

The Polish stationmaster at Sobibor, a man who looks and acts like a pedantic grammar-school teacher, tells in the film how labor details of Jews were first brought in to build the camp. "We thought it would be a sort of labor camp. Early in June, the first transport arrived, accompanied by SS troops in black uniforms. It was in the afternoon just after I had finished work. There were screams and groans in German, crying, whining, a lot of noise. When I came back to work the next morning, it was already absolutely quiet. I had no idea they were involved in the total extermination of all the Jews. I asked myself: Where are they? Where did they put all those Jews? All was quiet. There was an idyllic silence."

Between Word and Picture

From a moving car the camera captures the smokestacks of the Ruhr Valley, the industrial heart of Germany both then and now. Huge conglomerates, industrial parks, conveyor belts, enormous cranes—steel, concrete, and smoke. Against the backdrop of these passing scenes, the narrator reads a German document dated June 5, 1942 (exactly twenty-five years later, the Six-Day War was to break out in Israel). This document is a technical blueprint for making alterations and improvements in the gassing trucks, on the basis of accumulated experience. "Ninety-seven thousand Jews have been processed in the trucks to date, but minor operating defects have been discovered and we recommend the following improvements. It would be desirable in future to install electric lights, shielded by a steel grill, in the ceiling of the truck. For it is dark in the car when the doors are closed, and when the exhaust gas begins to be piped in, the result has been panic and loud screams, which made the work of the drivers more difficult and may attract undesirable attention. We also recommend the installation of properly graduated drains in the floor of the truck, because those who are being asphyxiated discharge bodily wastes during the course of the procedure, which lasts approximately 15–25 minutes. The cleanup between operations consumes unnecessary time. In addition, it is desirable to make the car shorter—although we are aware of the concern expressed by the engineers regarding the increased pressure on the front axle. There is no need for concern about overweight on the front axles of the trucks, for the merchandise, without exception, is pushed together during the journey and, for understandable psychological reasons, pressed to the locked doors at the rear end, so that the weight will nevertheless be well distributed on both axles. In order to save time, the above improvements should be made only when the trucks are otherwise out of service due to periodic overhauls."

You pause and reflect on the style of this document. Was Hannah Arendt right, after all, when she said that the greatest murder in all history was carried out by little gray people who knew not what they did? Is this not the language of bureaucratic nothingness, of a petty technocrat coping with a task to the best of his petty ability?

Or was Mr. Sammler, in Saul Bellow's novel, right when he rebuked Hannah Arendt, saying that every man knows what murder is and that the grayness is just a cover?

Distortion of language is what paved the way for this murder. Generations before the birth of Hitler, mass murderers already knew that you must first corrupt the words before you can corrupt those who use these words, so that they may be capable of murder in the guise of purification, cleaning, and healing. One who calls his enemy an "animal," "parasite," "louse," "beast of prey," or "germ" trains hearts for murder.

The German dictionary of destruction—"solution," "final solution," "training for productive work," "resettlement," "treatment," "special treatment," even the most explicit term used, "Vernichtung" (annihilation)—still calls to mind mice or termites, not human beings.

The Jewish dictionary of shudders—"Holocaust," "sheep to the slaughter," "raging foe," "oppressor," "Amalek," "the Nazi beast," and even, and always in the same breath, "Holocaust and heroism"—all these words attempt to bypass, to soften, to prettify, to console, or to place everything into one known familiar historic pattern: "Pharaoh," "wicked," "Haman," "Cossacks," "pogroms," "anti-Semites."

Therefore, when we wake up each morning, we should check the words in the newspaper as well as the words in our own mouths. We must treat words like hand grenades.

The murderer Franz Suchomel, who has a heart condition, responded to Lanzmann's entreaties and sang for him (and for the hidden camera and tape recorder) the anthem of the unit that carried out the murders. It was a hymn to duty, praise for those who obeyed even when obedience was difficult and frightening, even when there was no prospect of glory. Lanzmann also persuaded Simon Srebnik, "the Chelmno nightingale," to sing some of the songs from those days. Suchomel's voice, in contrast to Srebnik's, is cracked. He doesn't sing well. The melody sounds ludicrously out of tune, and the murderer heartily apologizes for it: "We are laughing now, but it's not right. Please, don't laugh at me. There's nothing to laugh at. All this is very sad. Not funny at all." (Neither of them had laughed.)

And afterward, pointer in hand, as though delivering a lecture, he elucidates, "for history's sake," how it was done, using an enlarged map of the Treblinka camp. "Treblinka was not large at all. Maybe five hundred meters at its widest point. And . . . eighteen thousand—that's an exaggeration. Abso-

159

lutely. We never reached eighteen thousand a day. On the busiest days, when they worked all night, maybe twelve or fifteen thousand went through. Not more. In each transport there were between thirty and fifty cars. They would divide them into groups of ten to twelve cars and take each group in to the platform inside the camp. The others waited their turn inside the cars. Lithuanian and Ukrainian guards sat on the roof of the cars. Bloodhounds, that's what they were. I tell you, they were the worst!

"In every shift there were three to five Germans, another ten Ukrainians and Lithuanians, and maybe twenty Jews. The Red Commando processed the clothes that the people took off."

Lanzmann: "How much time elapsed between the unloading, the undressing, and the liquidation?"

Suchomel: "Women—one hour. The whole train—two hours. Within two hours it was all finished. You couldn't wait long. It was cold as hell. Fifteen or twenty degrees below zero, sometimes. Those poor things were even colder. They were naked."

The "tunnel," or the "tube," was a path covered over with barbed wire, camouflaged with pine branches. Special details of Jews would bring fresh branches from the woods each morning. According to Suchomel, the Jews called this tube *Himmelweg*—"the path to heaven." According to one Jewish witness, some Germans called the tube by the same name. So we have a little copyright dispute here.

"The men," says Suchomel, "had to be beaten hard so they would walk into the tube. But women were not beaten."

"Why?" asks Lanzmann.

Suchomel looks at him with total incomprehension.

"Why weren't the women beaten?"

Astonishment spreads across the aging Nazi's face. He is

silent. His features express shock. How can a civilized person ask such a question? How could anyone have such ugly thoughts? Finally, he breaks his silence and says, "I don't know. I never went near there—near the women, that is. Lithuanians and Ukrainians were there. You couldn't get close. They were naked. Besides, they relieved themselves right then and there. Out of fear of death. Todesangst. It is perfectly natural, from a scientific point of view. For example, my own mother, who died in her own bed, while she was dying, got up and did it at the foot of the bed." Suchomel gestures with his hands, illustrating a little heap. And then there comes a strange, amazing moment of manly kinship between Lanzmann and Suchomel, a kinship deriving from the fact that both of them are cultured people who know that it isn't nice to use vulgar language and that there are limits established by universal good taste, limits that must not be transgressed. It is simply not done. Lanzmann accompanies his next question with an up-and-down motion of both hands, without words (meaning, did the women do it standing up?). Suchomel answers Lanzmann with a nod of his head and the same movement of his hands (meaning, yes, standing up). A moment later he corrects himself, "No. No. Not standing up. Why standing up? No. No. They could . . . squat."

These things, and others like them, can be captured only by a camera: the embarrassment, the silences, and the body language. The film gives full expression to several cinematic possibilities. There are dozens of minutes of silence, of unanswered questions, of unsolicited answers, of embarrassment, squirming, and evasiveness, of stammering and playacting, hand and body gestures, mimicry and laughter. Yes, laughter, too, and trembling lips and open weeping.

And there are many minutes of freight trains standing, moving, stopping, by night with frightening headlights, by day, and at dusk. The camera ignores many of the generally accepted rules of "cinematic syntax," such as orderly modulations, deleting background noises, editing out various stutters, shortening "empty" minutes, and giving special attention to "quality" or "uniformity." On the other hand, most of the ten hours are hours of face-to-face talks or silence or contorted faces. It seems that the victims, the murderers, and the witnesses, along with the interviewer, all suffer from "verbal insufficiency." No language is adequate (although the characters in the film use any of six or seven languages). But the language of the film is the language of photographed silence; the language of pursed lips and gaping, speechless mouths; the language of never-ending freight trains, and the language of snowscapes of barren fields. The dark green language of the Polish winter and the clear dazzling blue summer language of the Tel Aviv seashore. The language of the skyscrapers of New York and the alleyways of Corfu; and more trains moving through the twilight and past station signs and Polish villages and the lake at Lausanne, the industrial plants of Germany, and an Israeli barbershop in the town of Holon; trains in the rain and in the sun, at night and during the day. It is impossible to imagine any way other than film by which this creation could have been produced.

Franz Suchomel's finale: "Children, the old, and the sick were taken directly to the infirmary in the woods. There was a big white flag with a big red cross on it. They went willingly. They believed they would be taken care of there. Suddenly they saw the ditch. It was full of burning corpses. They were ordered to undress and to sit on a sort of ramp. Here [he indicates the spot on the map of Treblinka]. That is where they each got a bullet in the back of the head. There was always a fire burning in the ditch. They would throw in wood, papers; they'd spill gasoline, rags; they'd throw in garbage and, of course, the people. People burn very well."

The murderers and the witnesses, Poles and Germans alike, use, almost exclusively, one grammatical form: the third person plural. Sometimes they use the passive voice: "were taken," "were beaten," "were transported," "were unloaded," "were treated."

Most of the Jews in the film also use the same grammatical forms. But not all of them, and not always. Some say "we" and "I." Not one of the Nazis in the film ever says "we took them," or even "we told them," or at least "they told us to transport them." The words "I" and "we" are uttered by the Germans only in tandem with the words "didn't know" or "didn't see."

Rudolf Vrba and Filip Müller, two Jews who had "worked" in Auschwitz and survived, describe the death factory in detail and sometimes in technical language. When the Jews were removed from the boxcars, a "preliminary sorting" was done. The dead—including those who pretended to be dead—were thrown by the Jewish Sonderkommando people into trucks and cremated in the ovens. Others, after the infamous "selection" of those able to work, were chased by whip lashes into the disrobing rooms. They were told they were going to have a shower and be disinfected. The disrobing rooms were adjacent to the gas chambers, where up to three thousand people could be asphyxiated at one time. Four crematoria were kept going almost around the clock to turn the bodies into ashes.

In the words of Rudolf Vrba, the disrobing rooms were like an "international information center." On the walls were signs in several languages. There were special hooks on which to hang clothes. There were also several wooden benches for the convenience of the "clients." The signs said, "Cleanliness Is Good," "Wash!," "Cleanliness Is Health," "Head Lice Can Kill!" The purpose of the signs, of course, was to keep up the illusion and extend the deception until the very last minute. The gas itself arrived at Auschwitz in tanker trucks marked with the symbol of the International Red Cross and the word "Disinfectant."

Thus, the inventor of this scheme of deception, of murder in the guise of a hygienic procedure, had no banal mind. We don't know whose idea it all was. But it undeniably contains a spark of originality. It seems that other means of deception could have been devised. For instance, the Jews could have been told that they were going to be taken to a registration office, or to some employment bureau, or to a lecture hall, as part of their "retraining." From among all these and other possibilities, the unknown "poet" chose the metaphor of hygiene: "shower," "soap," "cleanliness," "delousing," "disinfection." So he had the wisdom of infinite cunning, extraordinary psychological subtlety, and a finely tuned sensitivity, to choose the most effective nuances. He chose to employ European values common to both the murderers and their victims, to exploit some universal urge for cleanliness, to touch upon a point on which the Jews, like every minority, were exceptionally sensitive, because of the age-old accusation leveled by racists at victims of racism: You are hated because you are dirty, because you stink, because you are carriers of disease. Take a bath, and then you can be worthy of us, of being accepted by us, even in our living rooms. There was infinite cunning behind the seductive German offer that was made to the Jews at the threshold of the "showers": "Enter as a (dirty) Jew, emerge as a (clean) human being."

Besides, after days in a boxcar, everyone would yearn for a bath, and truly need one. Therefore, they could imagine they saw a clear logic, a sanitary justification—for the good of all concerned—in the idea of showers and disinfection. Result: They marched in almost willingly, maybe they even marched in gladly.

Millions of human beings arrived in this fashion—quiet, naked, deceived, and hoping for the best—at the gas chambers. "The gas," Filip Müller relates, "was introduced in the form of crystals. The lights were turned off. A fierce battle broke out in the dark. The strong climbed on top of the weak. Driven by the blind instinct of self-preservation, they surged toward the doors—and toward the ceiling. Parents stepped on their children. They tore each other to pieces with their fingernails. When the doors were opened and the gas was pumped out, and we had to enter and remove them fast, we found them all twisted, trampled, covered with blood, urine, and feces. . . ."

Intimidation, attrition, deception—these were not by-products of the plot of destruction, but, rather, crucial components of its effectiveness. A single woman carrying a child and bursting into hysterical screams, thus stirring panic in the crowd, was enough to slow down the entire "procedure." It was imperative to bring them into the asphyxiation chamber in a quiet, submissive state. Starved, thirsty, exhausted, half-crazed from the horrors of the terrible journey, the dogs, the floodlights, the shouts, the blows, and the gunfire, they arrived at the platforms begging for water and, perhaps with their last bit of strength, grateful for the "offer" of a shower. "There was no point in warning them," Müller says. "Why turn their last moments into horror? To deprive them of vain hope? How would it have helped them to know that in a few minutes they would be dead? Once, a Sonderkommando member met a woman here whom he knew well. He whispered to her that she and all the other passengers in the transport would soon be turned into ashes. The woman ran like a maniac to warn the other women. They didn't believe her. They told her she'd gone out of her mind. They refused to listen. She screamed and raked herself with her fingernails. Maybe she really had gone mad from shock and despair. And how did it all end? Everyone went to the gas chamber—except for this one woman. The Germans subjected the woman to hellish tortures until she broke down and pointed out the Sonderkommando man who had revealed the truth to her. They threw him, live, into the oven. That's why we didn't tell them."

"I didn't know a thing," says Walter Steier, a former Nazi party member who was director-general of the Reich Railroad Authority for the eastern areas. "I was glued to my desk day and night. I never went outdoors. I did not see the transports. Department 33 was in charge of the Sonderzüge [special trains] and supplied trains and schedules at the request of the Gestapo in Berlin. At group fares. Yes, I had some idea that many of these special trains went to Treblinka and Auschwitz. But how was I to know what they were carrying? Or what was going to happen to the cargo there? This was not my department. Yes, there were all kinds of rumors. Rumors always circulate in wartime. They said they were transporting Jews or criminals or that sort of people, in these trains. Of course it was better not to talk about it. I knew nothing. Ach nein! Ach, Gott im Himmel, nein."

The Moral and the
Yoke of Guilt

And the mob assembled in a crowd
Carrying the yoke of guilt
To hang it upon lords and king
Lest it remain on its own neck.

    —NATAN ALTERMAN,
     "Poems of the Plagues of Egypt"

One of the most "uncinematic" portions of *Shoah* is etched
in my memory as one of the most piercing scenes I have ever
seen on film. For a full quarter of an hour, the historian Raul
Hilberg sits in his nice study at his home in Vermont (trees
and snow out the window, books, a lamp, a desk) and explains
to Claude Lanzmann the contents of a typed German document, about fifteen lines long, the essence of which is a list
of serial numbers. Hilberg is the historian who apparently
served as Hannah Arendt's inspiration for her theory about the
"banality of evil." Many people accuse him of insulting the
memory of the victims by attributing to them and to their
leaders perverse obedience and cowardly submission, while

describing the murderers as "simple people who had no special wickedness in them." (See the fiery 1964 brochure by K. Shabtai called *Like Sheep to the Slaughter?* The historian Lucy Davidowicz, though in a less emotional tone, likewise categorically rejects Hilberg's position.)

The document is an order form for Train No. 587, from the Gestapo in Berlin to the Reich Railroad Authority. Classification: "Internal." This is the lowest security classification. Hilberg proceeds to explain: "The psychological key to the whole operation was: Never use explicit terms. Trivialize, as much as possible, the significance of the murder operation. Even in the eyes of the murderers themselves." The low security classification of this document is evident also from the fact that it bore no fewer than eight or nine addresses. Every railroad station on the way from Radom to Warsaw and Treblinka and from there to Częstochowa and back to Treblinka, and so on, needed a copy in order to be forewarned that this special train would be passing through. The train in question is a "freight train" bound for Treblinka and an empty train on its way back from Treblinka. Fifty cars. Leaving Zhidachov at 4:18 P.M. and arriving at Treblinka at 11:24 A.M. the following day, September 30, 1941. Leaving Treblinka, after the "run," at 3:49 P.M. on the same day, arriving at another town at three o'clock the next morning and again back to Treblinka and again leaving, this time for Częstochowa and around again. All this is still the same train, but its serial number changes with each run.

The title of the document is "Order for Long-Range Transportation Planning." Hilberg quietly explains: "In this piece of paper, we are talking about perhaps forty thousand dead Jews: four or five transports times fifty cars times perhaps one hundred and fifty people in each car. And this is the original document. This piece of paper was held by the bureaucrats as well. And this is all that remains. The dead no longer exist."

The Railroad Authority would transport anything for a fee, Hilberg explains. The Gestapo was charged for "charter travel," exactly the way groups of workers, for instance, were charged for package vacation trips to the Alps. At the group fare, children under the age of four traveled free, those up to the age of ten at half price. The tickets purchased were one-way, of course, except in the case of the guards, for whom the Gestapo bought round-trip tickets. If there was any dirt in the cars, or if the cars had been damaged (approximately ten percent of the passengers died en route), the Railroad Authority sent a special bill to the Gestapo. In several instances, credit was extended. The accounting methods were in keeping with methods that had been established for generations. Sometimes the complicated system involved currency-exchange proce-dures. The Gestapo in Greece might receive, as in the spring of 1943, a bill from the Railroad Authority for two million marks for the transfer of forty-six thousand Greek Jews to Po-land. However, the Gestapo office in Greece could not make payment in German Marks, or in Yugoslav or Polish currency, depending on what countries the trains passed through, be-cause the Athens Gestapo office had at its disposal only Greek drachmas, expropriated from the bank accounts of the depor-tees. (Hilberg emphasized to Lanzmann one basic principle: There was no budget for the extermination.) How, then, was such a problem solved? Wasn't it forbidden to possess foreign currency in wartime Greece? Well, it transpires that the com-mon cliché of the "pedantic" German bureaucrat is not always true. In this particular case, the German bureaucracy was not at all rigid or obtuse: the Railroad Authority simply agreed to forgo payment. In contrast to the prevailing myth, it turns out that in exceptional cases, even the German bureaucracy was

169

capable of flexibility, or even generosity. Or both of these weaknesses at the same time.

How is all this different from a "conventional" pogrom? There are no rowdy Cossacks, drinking themselves senseless, then roaming about to pillage and rape and slaughter to their heart's desire. This time there is no element of lust. There are no axes, no murderous eyes. There is only order.

Filip Müller, the Sonderkommando member who survived Auschwitz, says: "When no transports arrived, we called it the 'dead season.' These were the most dangerous periods for us. They would send us to the infirmary and cure us with one pill [a bullet in the back of the neck]. We were very much afraid of these 'dead seasons.' "

The last quarter of the film leads, indirectly but persistently, to the Warsaw ghetto uprising. There is testimony about preparations for a rebellion in Treblinka (where a daring, courageous uprising did finally take place); testimony about a plan to rebel and sabotage the "production line" in Auschwitz. To this end it was necessary to wait for a new shipment of Jews who were not yet half dead. "And indeed, when the Greek Jews arrived," says Richard Glazar, who was in the Sonderkommando at Treblinka, "we decided that the time had come. They were healthy and strong. David Brot said to me, 'Look! The Maccabees have arrived in Treblinka.' But these particular Maccabees simply refused to rebel, because they refused to believe what was in store for them. In the end, this was one of the smoothest exterminations—it went so quickly with them. . . .

"We hoped," says Glazar, "to attack the guards in January

1943, to take their guns, to occupy the headquarters, destroy the facilities, and then escape. We didn't succeed. The transports almost stopped. They began to starve us. And as a result of this starvation, we were hit by a typhoid epidemic. . . . Yet, despite it all, there was an uprising in Treblinka, and some Nazis paid with their lives."

Filip Müller: "Thousands arrived each day . . . thousands. . . . We were busy all the time. . . . We felt there were no more human beings left. . . . Humanity had deserted us."

Then comes the story of the Warsaw ghetto uprising. Kajek, now a member of Kibbutz Lohamei Hagetta'ot (this kibbutz near Acre, founded by ghetto fighters, has a Holocaust museum), was sent to get help from the "Aryan side," to ask for guns from the Polish underground. They turned him away. He and his comrade returned to the ghetto through the sewers. But there was nothing left. It was all over. Except for a strange, illusory female voice, the source of which Kajek tried at length to locate—without success. He says, "I felt that I was the last human being, that there were no more people in the world."

There is no lesson, no moral, no yoke of guilt. The film ends with a very long shot of a very long freight train traveling through the twilight.

In his 1979 book *Jew-Hatred: From Religious Hatred to Racial Rejection*, the historian Jacob Katz says, "Like any constellation that derives from more than one cause, this was a

171

unique constellation, and it is unlikely to recur in this form. Moreover, even if all the causes of the first constellation were to recur, the circumstances would be different because they would include an unavoidable reaction to the results of the previous constellation. Which will, of necessity, break the overlapping pattern. Therefore, any attempt to predict the future on the basis of precedents from the past is doomed to failure."

True. But what is the "unavoidable reaction to the results of the previous constellation"?

"We must have a strong military." "We must not rely on might." "We must preserve our humanity." "We must not be too humane in this brutal world." "We must fight racism." "We must destroy the new Amalek before it destroys us." "Auschwitz proved that there is no God." "Auschwitz proved that we have sinned against God and must repent." "The lesson of Auschwitz is that the Jews must never again be concentrated in one place." "The lesson of Auschwitz is that the Jews must not be scattered among the Gentiles." "Auschwitz was the rotten fruit of the Germanic spirit / of Christian tradition / of Western civilization." "Auschwitz was the ultimate conclusion of Jewish life in the diaspora and of existence without an independent state of their own." "Auschwitz could happen anywhere; no people is immune from the Nazi virus, not even we ourselves."

And so on, ad infinitum.

Claude Lanzmann's film *Shoah* says a great deal less: "Auschwitz was." And also: "Auschwitz was not incomprehensible. The camera and the words and the silences are capable of comprehending."

And also: "The past is still present. Nothing has ended. Here is the murderer and here is the victim who survived this murderer. Here are the witnesses, here was the place, and here is where it was done, and this is exactly how it was done."

INTERVIEWEE: "It is impossible to talk about it. Leave me alone. It is hard for me. It is impossible."

INTERVIEWER: "I understand. Forgive me. But continue. Carry on. You must."

> Serialized in *Davar*,
> June 27, 1986,
> to July 6, 1986

Of Gentle Austria
and the Elders of Zion

What did Dr. Kurt Waldheim, that righteous gentleman, do during World War II?

According to his accusers, and according to the various documents published recently, the former secretary general of the United Nations was a junior partner in such war crimes as the hunting, capture, and murder of partisan fighters, the massacre of hostages, the incineration of entire villages together with their populations. Not with his own delicate hands, heaven forbid; just indirectly. Only as a small cog in the wheel. Only by way of doing his patriotic duty and fulfilling the sacred oath he had sworn to the Führer.

Whereas, according to his version, the good doctor had devoted himself during those evil years only to the pure art of translation, as high-minded youth, everywhere, are wont to devote themselves to art for art's sake. And in his bed at night, he would shed silent tears in overwhelming horror at Nazi atrocities, which he, of course, had never seen or, as he swore on his honor as a German officer, even heard about or been able to hear about.

And what did Austria, his homeland, do during those same years?

It became the victim, the first victim, of the German machine of oppression. It suffered under the heel of the Nazi boot and secretly dreamed of the coming liberation.

A fascinating, sophisticated repression mechanism has enabled the citizens of this small, musical, peace-loving country to forget or to repress the Austrian origins of Adolf Hitler, Adolf Eichmann, and of tens of thousands of other zealous Nazis, and to portray themselves as victims. Someone came from Uzbekistan (or was it from the Fiji Islands?), penetrated the heart of civilized Europe, and, until they managed to stop him, succeeded, most regrettably, in raping Poland and Holland, in dishonoring Czechoslovakia and France, in forcing Belgium and Yugoslavia into submission, and at the very outset of his frenzy he robbed beautiful, righteous Austria of her moral virginity. These and other explanations can be heard to this day from polite, well-mannered, middle-aged Viennese. When you listen to these Austrian sob stories you almost catch yourself beginning to wonder why those dear Austrians, our brothers in distress, did not do as we did, why they have not yet presented Germany with an angry demand for reparations. But perhaps President Kurt Waldheim, taught by his own experience of Germany's deeds, will present just such a claim to his northern neighbor, and, under the slogan "Remember what Amalek has done unto you," he will neither desist nor rest until the Federal Republic of West Germany has compensated Austria for all its sufferings.

For forty years, West Germany has made notable efforts to come to terms with its past, as seen from the courageous address delivered by President Richard von Weizsäcker in 1986. Has anyone heard of a similar effort in Austria? Moreover, a handful, though a heartbreakingly small handful, of brave Germans stood up and sacrificed their lives in several unsuccessful attempts to overthrow Hitler's regime. Has anyone ever heard of such an attempt in beautiful Austria? The worldwide campaign to expose Kurt Waldheim's Nazi past, we are told, only helped him, by raising his political stock with his electorate. Once again we hear muffled, dark murmurings in Austria about an international Jewish conspiracy and about the crafty machinations of the Elders of Zion. Approximately half of Waldheim's countrymen voted for him, not despite his past, but because of it, not in spite of the worldwide campaign to expose what he did while wearing the Nazi uniform, but precisely because of that campaign. One has the impression that many Austrians would like, once again, to teach "international Jewry" a lesson it won't forget. The election of the translator-doctor thus becomes nothing less than an Austrian plebiscite on the meaning of Austria's past.

If the Austrians will indeed say "Yea" to their past, then it is the duty of the victims to say an unambiguous "Nay" to the Austrians: Greece and Yugoslavia, the coalition of nations that fought against the Nazis, and, last but not least, West Germany, which has invested certain intellectual and moral efforts in turning over a new leaf, ought to make some far-reaching response to what is a potentially neo-Nazi result of the Austrian plebiscite.

As for the Jewish state, it must certainly not evade the necessary conclusions: Diplomatic relations between Vienna and Jerusalem must be suspended at least until Dr. Waldheim's term of office ends.

Let no Israeli ambassador present his credentials to a man who had a hand in Nazi atrocities and who was elected to office by virtue of his shady past—lest the shades of the Jewish Elders of Zion who were forced in 1938 by the enthusiastic electors of Dr. Waldheim to sweep the lovely sidewalks of Vienna with their beards appear at the ceremony; lest they appear and with their charred beards sweep away the recipient of the credentials along with him who presents them.

Davar, June 8, 1986

IN THE HOUSE OF
A HANGED MAN . . .

Exercises of a
Sick Imagination

(On April 12, 1984, a civilian bus on a routine trip from Tel Aviv
to Ashkelon was hijacked by terrorists, who threatened to kill their
hostages. Israeli armed forces stormed the bus and succeeded in
capturing two terrorists alive. The hijackers were allegedly killed later
that night in the course of interrogation by agents of the Israeli secret
service. After a public outcry, the heads of the service were forced
to resign, but were granted a pre-trial pardon by the president of the
State of Israel.)

Pandora's Box

Standard operating procedures: Whenever a dispute arises over
the moral norms in our war with the Arabs, certain spokesmen
from the right stand up to condemn the hypocrisy of the moderates. Again and again they argue that we are all "equally
tainted." Was Arab land stolen? Why, kibbutzim, too, were
established on Arab land. Was the Arab population expelled?
Why, Berl Katznelson, the éminence grise of the Labor Zionist
movement before the emergence of the state, once proposed
an exchange of populations. Were innocent civilians massa-
cred? Why, "your boys" sometimes killed civilians, too. Were
prisoners murdered? Why, you did that, too. Have there been
instances of torture? Why, you also did such things. You want
to investigate what happened in the attack on the bus on the
way to Ashkelon? Go right ahead. For our part, we'll investigate
who gave the order to bomb the Jordanian town of Irbid in
1970. This standard operating procedure is completely identical with the well-known technique of Israel's enemies, who

strive to portray Zionism as an ongoing crime and all Zionists as criminals. If you don't agree to buy our brutal norms, say some speakers on the right, we will open up and smear the entire Zionist undertaking from its very foundations. Either you agree with us to abide by a gangsters' code of honor, or we will open "Pandora's Box" and blow the House of Israel sky-high.

This argument can be refuted with the utmost simplicity: There are no bloodless wars. In the seventy-year war between ourselves and the Arabs there were several sad incidents of which we ought to be ashamed. That's a fact. And what should be our conclusion? The moderates say we have to fight to make certain that such incidents do not happen again. Some voices from the right, on the other hand, contend that we have to turn these incidents into the norm. All is fair in war, they say, so you bleeding hearts just shut up.

The Know-Nothings

There are arguments now to the effect that the "regime by investigative commissions" is undermining national security. This argument is the product of a sick imagination. The truth is that on more than one occasion the security of the state has been harmed by the system of "leaks" and loose lips, a system which is not a by-product of the investigative and judicial systems, but primarily a disease of politicians. The right-wing spokesmen who exalt security are among the main contributors to the difficulty in keeping even real secrets secret around here.

In addition, it is argued that the sword of investigation that hangs over the heads of our soldiers and policymakers is the cause of the "know-nothing syndrome"; that our soldiers are afraid to take the initiative without a lawyer by their side. This argument, too, is the fruit of imagination run riot. The truth is this: The brainwashing philosophy according to which it is forbidden during periods of national emergency to think, to protest, or to engage in debates on moral standards—and anyone who doubts this is culpable of treason, subversion, and defeatism—is the mother of "know-nothingism." It seeks to trample freedom of thought and initiative. A society that does not tolerate any debate on moral issues, that stigmatizes any debater as a traitor, will inevitably turn into a narrow-minded society of know-nothings.

The Know-Everythings

A theoretical exercise of a sick imagination: What is Israel's most zealously guarded security secret? Imagine, for a moment, the following most confidential secret: Yasir Arafat is an Israeli agent, whose real Hebrew name is Issar Arif, who was planted, as a mole, deep in the enemy camp thirty years ago, managed to become the leader of the terrorist organization, and in that position actually succeeded in causing damage and creating havoc in the Palestinian movement. Imagine that last year, while on home leave, Yasir-Issar was on a bus bound for Ashkelon on his way to visit his wife and children. Imagine that the terrorists who hijacked the bus recognized him. Imagine further that, when they were captured, the two murderers threatened to expose the real identity of the greatest secret agent of all time. Imagine that, in order to prevent this disclosure, the Israeli secret security forces put the two captured terrorists to death. Imagine that the head of the internal security service, Mr. Avraham Shalom, had, or had not, given the order to do this, and that Prime Minister Yitzhak Shamir did, or did not, know about it. Imagine that by killing the two terrorists hundreds of human lives were saved, and the disclosure of the true identity of Our Man in the PLO was prevented. Imagine that, in order to protect this historic secret, witnesses perjured, or did not perjure, themselves, and attempts were, or were not, made to suborn testimony, and that there was, or was not, a cover-up, collusion, and libel. Just imagine all that.

Even in a fantastic scenario of this sort, there is no point in a pretrial pardon and no justification for blocking an investigation. It is still possible to appoint a two-man commission consisting of, let us say, the head of the Supreme Court, Chief Justice Meir Shamgar, and the former head of Mossad, Yitzhak Hofi. This commission will hear the evidence, and consider and understand the crucial importance of the Arafat secret. Then perhaps it will deliver a verdict of sixteen words: "There was no alternative to the acts that were committed. We therefore exonerate all those involved."

The Root of the Controversy

But what if it should turn out that the leaders of Likud insist that the question of a pretrial pardon is a question of principle and values, of one standard versus another, of one code of ethics versus another, one philosophy versus another, the principle of a nation of law versus the principle of the-only-good-Arab-is-a-dead-Arab, the principle of equality for all before the law versus the principle of a privileged few above the law, the principle of honest accountability versus the principle of the sacred lie? Well, if that is the case, we ought to hold new and one-issue general elections immediately.

Davar, July 4, 1986

In the House of
a Hanged Man . . .

It seems that the Ashkelon bus incident will eventually be investigated, either by a Commission on Judicial Inquiry or by ordinary—albeit in camera—police and judicial means. This is all as it should be. Whatever the results of the investigation and the proceedings, it is clear that this affair has again exposed the intensity of the dispute raging here, not between security and law, not between Likud and Labor, but between supporters and opponents of the principle that the end justifies the means.

Israel's military strength grew out of shadowy beginnings. NILI and "Hashomer," the Haganah and the Palmach, the Irgun and the Stern group were all initially underground organizations, during Ottoman or British rule. An underground, any underground, is a challenge to the law. However, its challenge is not a manifestation of anarchism, but is made on the basis of another law.

From the outset there were fierce arguments, usually, but not always, conducted in whispers among the fighting men in the various underground organizations, their commanders, and their ideologists over the question: What is a nation fighting for its existence permitted or forbidden to do in the use of force? Sometimes the argument seemed to focus on issues of expediency and gain: Does it, or does it not, pay to use personal terror against the alien overlords? Is it, or is it not, worthwhile to kill Arabs indiscriminately? Is it, or is it not, to our advantage to attack women and children? At other times the argument seemed to center on the question of the limits of internal discipline: Is it permitted, or forbidden, to condone "irregular acts" against the enemy? Is it permitted, or forbidden, to disobey the authority of the "political echelon" when that echelon takes a position that some may regard as appeasing, "soft," waffling, or even traitorous? Sometimes the argument was clothed in the guise of morality: Is a concept like "the morality of war" self-contradictory? Is the juxtaposition of the words "purity of arms" mutually exclusive?

These, among others, were the arguments in those bygone days. Since then the State of Israel has been established; its army has emerged from underground, although its secret branches continue to operate in the shadows; from time to time, various parties in the old disputes have managed to switch position and principles, in accordance with the politics of the moment or passing personal considerations. We have heard former right-wing "secessionists" lambaste the left for holding meetings with the PLO, claiming it is intolerable that individuals should conduct private foreign policy; conversely, we have heard objectors to the evacuation of Sinai rebuke the objectors to the war in Lebanon, and objectors to the war in Lebanon criticize the objectors to the evacuation of Sinai, reminding one another that the law stands above all or, alternatively, that individual conscience stands above the law, or, instead, that the security of the state takes precedence over

186

conscience and law alike, or, conversely, that the value of life
or of the commandments of the Bible takes precedence over
law, conscience, and security, or all three.

But the root of the controversy has remained with us from
those past days down to the present, and will into the future:
Is a nation surrounded by enemies permitted to engage in
anything, including acts conventionally defined as war crimes,
in order to overcome its enemies? Do despicable, criminal
methods of warfare employed by the enemy justify the use of
despicable, criminal methods of warfare by us in return? In
times of war should morality, just like women and children,
be left at home?

In short: Does the end justify the means? Does it justify
all means? Does it always justify all means? Does every end
justify all means all the time? And, if not, how and where do
you draw the line? How easy and convenient to blur this
argument and to envelop it in mist! This is usually done with
the help of the little pat phrase "It all depends." War crimes?
It depends against whom. Massacres of civilians? It depends
on which civilians and under what circumstances. What about
trampling the law underfoot? It depends on the benefits that
will result. What about trampling conscience underfoot in the
name of blind obedience? It depends on whose conscience.

This is not a dispute between "the committed" and "the
gutless" and certainly not between "hawks" and "doves." It is
not difficult to see that on the fringes of the left, too, there
are people for whom the end justifies the means. Nor is this
a controversy over "our image" or "our reputation." This is a
controversy over the meaning and purpose of life itself. The
end-justifies-the-means camp hints to us, time after time, that
we had better take a leaf from the book of our enemy, who is
not selective about choosing his means. That we ought to learn

lessons in savagery from Russia, Syria, and the PLO—and perhaps there is something to be learned even from the Nazis— provided that we are careful to wrap this catechism of ours into a thick bulletproof vest of false piety, hypocrisy, and self-righteous slogans. In opposition to proponents of such views, there always have been those who contend that we are forbidden to adopt the murderous methods of the enemy, that we are forbidden, unconditionally and without "it depends," to be war criminals, even when war criminals seek to destroy us. And if there have been some war criminals among us—and there have been—we must isolate and denounce them and not turn their "precedents" into the norm. It is forbidden to commit war crimes—and not because "crime doesn't pay." (The savagery and brutality of the enemy have, thus far, taken him only from defeat to defeat. This is worth remembering. The crimes of our enemies did not pay.) No. It is forbidden simply because it is forbidden. Period. This is an axiom. And it is forbidden because whoever fights his enemies by the rule that the end justifies all means is ultimately bound to apply that rule also to other areas of life—or of death. A person who claims—even in a narrow, well-defined area—that "anything goes" is sick. The juxtaposition of the words "anything goes," like the juxtaposition of the words "it depends on," will not stop with the bullet-riddled bodies of the terrorists who had surrendered in the dunes of Ashkelon after hijacking a bus. And it will not stop with the bodies of Arabs who are not terrorists but simply "superfluous." Nor at the bodies of certified non-Arabs. Indeed, not at the body of anyone. The essence of the words "anything goes" and "it depends on" is their contagious nature. Anyone who has crossed, even for the sake of an exalted goal, the boundary line of the most basic universal principles of morality, anyone who has entered the

shadowy, tainted area above which, in the words of an Israeli
court of justice, there "flies a black flag of an order that is
clearly illegal," anyone who has given, or obeyed, such an
order, is liable to return from there infected, and, in everything
he does, he is liable to behave in accordance with the theory
"it all depends."

Some time ago, Israeli General Yosef Geva related that
during the Camp David peace talks he was approached by the
raving right-wing poet Uri Zvi Greenberg, who begged him
to volunteer to kill Menachem Begin in order to "save the
country from total destruction." ("Why me?" asked General
Geva. "Because they will never suspect you!" replied the fiery
poet, who believed with all his heart that the end justified all
means.) In the poet's view, this idea was entirely logical: The
taking of the life of Menachem Begin, who would give up
the Sinai Peninsula, had to be weighed against the rescue of
the nation from destruction. "The damage caused by Begin is
a thousand times greater than the damage done by all of the
terrorists put together."

As we know, Geva chose to forgo the honor and he did
not save the nation. Meanwhile, Uri Zvi Greenberg has passed
away. Menachem Begin keeps his silence and floats over us
all like a crescent moon. But the country is full of people who
declare (at least in whispers) that the nation is in danger and
that the end of saving it justifies all means; that "when you
are at war, act like it"; that the definition of crime depends on
the identity of its victim. Among all these "justifiers" there are
not a few who think that left-wing M. K. Yossi Sarid is worse
than Arafat, that Shimon Peres is more dangerous than terrorist
leader Ahmed Jibril, or that Ezer Weisman is the chief agent
or perhaps the nephew of Syria's President Assad. Depending
on one's perspective, the same person can embody disaster or

salvation. Somewhere on the edges of the lunatic fringe there may be someone who regards Moshe Arens, Ariel Sharon, or Prime Minister Shamir as dangerous leftists who ought to be eliminated. If the rule is that the end indeed justifies the means and that "it all depends," then the survival of everything and everyone here is hanging by a thread.

There is a vicious but logically consistent straight line from the theory of "the end justifies all means" to the idea that "the only good Arab is a dead Arab" and the revelation that "some Jews are more dangerous to us than the Arabs." From here there is only a short distance to the grave of Emil Grunzweig, and from Emil's grave to the grave of a sick society which neither knows how to protect itself from the virus, nor dares to do so. To protect itself, precisely, on an extremely uncomfortable and embarrassing battlefield, the field where the bodies of two terrorist murderers lay, apparently shot after they had raised their arms in surrender.

If the end justifies all means, then the death of those two terrorists is small change indeed. But from their death it is only a short, inevitable path to what comes next. This plague can spread as plagues usually do. The sacred end continues unblinkingly to justify more and more means. False reports lead to attempts to suborn witnesses, which in turn lead to perjured testimony, which weaves a conspiracy of misjudgment and cover-up and whitewash and pretrial pardons in the dark of night and a verbal war to the death against domestic "traitors"—a war that will not remain verbal, because it is tied to the logic that the end justifies and the rule that it all depends. Thus there is no, nor can there ever be, compromise with the notion that the end justifies the means. By its own internal logic it will continue to justify additional means all along the way, until, at last, as we read in history books, both the end and the means will lie strewn over the battlefield, and so will we.

"In the house of a hanged man," goes the old saying, "do not talk of rope." At the scene of a crime, never say, "It depends."

Davar, July 18, 1986

THE DREAMS

A New Heart

Through most of history, the Jews have usually adopted two spiritual reference points: the distant, glorious past and some sort of distant messianic future. The present and the immediate future were almost always viewed as a "vale of tears," whose tribulations could be bemoaned but not acted upon; accordingly, it was considered pointless to spend too much emotional energy on them. It was assumed that when the Messiah came he would bring about the exalted future—thus renewing the marvelous past and at the same time dissipating the troubles of the present.

The Hebrew word *lefanim* carries two opposite connotations: "before" (in space), but "backward" (in time). In the latter sense, it is generally translated "in the past" or "of old"— for example, "Of old Thou didst lay the foundation of the earth" (Psalms 102:26). By contrast, the Hebrew word *aharey*, which bears a forward-looking significance in time ("after"), is closely related to the word *ahor*, whose spatial reference ("behind") looks back.

It may seem, then, that the temporal and spatial referents

of the Hebrew language are inherently contradictory; and that the Jews, throughout most of their history, have been "facing backward." Yet, in my own childhood and adolescence—years of fervent Zionist activity—nearly everyone concentrated on the present and the near future. Zionist society was a future-oriented society; as one of its anthems states, "Yesterday is gone and far behind us/ But tomorrow still lies far ahead."

Tomorrow Is Gone and Far behind Us

Now, we have returned to our former status as a past-oriented society. Tomorrow "is gone and far behind us"—and yesterday dominates all aspects of our lives. All around us, people are almost compulsively occupying themselves with the past— whether the very distant past or the recent past—and with such questions as who said what, in which argument, and which of them was right. The Bible, a source of inspiration for in-novators and reformers during the good years of the Zionist revolution, is becoming an authorization for stagnation, for objection to change, for abstention from the present, and for adoption of a backward-facing mental stance.

From that standpoint, there is something refreshing in the very title that Lova Eliav selected for his recent book: *New Heart, New Spirit*. He is the sort of person who chooses to face the future. Even when such persons delve into the past— whether to write their memoirs or, as in this case, to study and peruse the Bible—their intention is not to re-create what has been or to call up ghosts, but to find, in the personal or national past, tools to place at the disposal of the present and the future.

The truth is that Zionism has always incorporated a sort of dialectical tension between profound longing for the long-lost beauty of yesteryear and burning ambition to turn over an

196

entirely new leaf in Israel. In matters both great and small that tension persisted between the urge to re-create and the urge to innovate; the names given by early Zionists to their children, their settlements, and their books bear witness to this covert struggle. In the biblical words "renew our days as of old" (Lamentations 5:21), which became a popular Zionist slogan, this dialectic can be seen quite clearly. There can be no renewal without our days as of old, and vice versa. This is almost the entire Zionist sensibility in a nutshell.

Nevertheless, Zionism was basically a revolutionary movement, a movement aimed at smashing outmoded conventions. This remains no less true even though, in our day, the tendency is to conceal this, to round off the corners, to "Judaize" the Zionist revolution, and to water down the sharp opposition between modern, secular Zionism and old-style Orthodox Judaism. Zionism was a revolt against the advancing stagnation in Judaism, against the rabbinical negation of all innovation and change.

For thousands of years, the Jews lived outside history, even in opposition to history. History was a "game" considered fit for Gentiles only, and no good Jew would dream of dirtying his hands with it. We Jews were supposed to live in humility, willingly accepting our sufferings, until the coming of the Messiah—like a bunch of disaster victims lying at the foot of a mountain and waiting for the tornado to pass. History, it was thought, would go away; eventually it would come to an end. Afterward, the Messiah would come and take us, in his miraculous chariot, back to the glorious past, to the days of the Temple and the Kingdoms of Israel, and even farther back, to the Garden of Eden. All we had to do was keep ourselves pure, avoid sin, bow our heads, and wait. As long, alas, as we were still surrounded by history, we could have only one temporal goal: to survive. To get through history unscathed.

Not to try to change it; not to try to shape its course; and, heaven forbid, not to be so impertinent before the Creator as to attempt to take history into our own hands. History, the Jews said for thousands of years, is something through which to suffer, like a protracted illness, and from which to emerge on the other side—right into the days of the Messiah, whose coming would cancel all history, restore us to our homeland, and bring us full redemption.

A Classic Zionist Act

The intent of Zionism was to smash that passive attitude. The revolt involved in so doing was by no means easy. A relatively small group of "licentious, impudent spurners of the Torah" decided to take history and the fate of the Jewish people into its own hands, to break up the long wait for the Messiah, and to take an active role in shaping the historical and political future.

The fledgling movement was faced by various and sundry opponents. Among them were those who waved the Bible and other holy writings, shouting, "The Torah forbids innovation!" and insisting that the generation of Jews in question was forbidden to do anything their ancestors had not done before them. In other words, they, too, were supposed to sit and wait humbly, meekly, and patiently for the coming of the Messiah; until that time, all they were permitted to do was to purify themselves, to suffer, and to pray. None of the customs of their long-dead forefathers could be changed. Only to those ancestors, not to future generations, were we to be held responsible. Our thoughts, words, and deeds must be identical to those of our deceased ancestors. Even our garments—no matter what the time, place, or climate—must be patterned on theirs. To deviate, to move away from any of this by a single step, was forbidden.

The struggle between the Zionist revolutionaries and the Orthodox keepers of the commandments was unique in that both sides drew arguments and proofs from the Bible and the holy writings. Zionism did not treat its Orthodox opponents as most revolutions treat their opponents. It did not tell them: "Take your holy writings and go to hell!" It did not proclaim its intent to destroy the old world to its very foundations. Rather, it sought to establish—and, indeed, succeeded in establishing—for itself a measure of legitimacy from the standpoint of its opponents. In other words, Zionism based its propositions on "their" texts, "their" sources, "their" sages. It argued that its intent was not to destroy the Jewish heritage, but to give it a new interpretation within the framework of the well-known, familiar, and legitimate interpretations shaped and reshaped by Jews throughout the course of time. Zionism, generally speaking, did not say that the Jewish heritage was none of our business. Rather, its position might be phrased thus: "We are the heirs, and it is our right to interpret, to stress new focal points, and to detract from the centrality of previous focal points—as the sages have done in every generation."

It may, therefore, be said that Lova Eliav, in his approach to the Bible, as delineated in his book *New Heart, New Spirit*, has performed a classic Zionist act. He interprets and stresses as he pleases—without, however, claiming any sort of exclusivity, without rejecting other interpretations, without denouncing other views or their proponents. The debate between Zionism and old-style Orthodox Judaism is not founded on the "rebels" throwing the Bible out the window, kicking over the traces of the Jewish heritage, and seeking to establish a new nation. On the contrary, it is based on the fact that the

199

Zionist "rebels" view themselves as the inheritors of a great library that had belonged to their fathers and grandfathers for a hundred generations. In their fathers' time, they state, some of the books in that library were housed on the nightstand, and others on a high shelf that could be reached only with a ladder. Their grandfathers also kept certain books in the cellar and others within closer reach. Their great-great-grandfathers, too, had priorities of their own. Thus, it may be seen that each generation has a right to rearrange the library, to place certain books on the top shelf and bring others within easy reach. This is Eliav's basic premise; it is similar to that of a man who walks through a field pointing out certain plants as edible or medicinal and others as poisonous. He is not trying to uproot the toxic growth, nor does he seek to ignore it, but, rather, to recognize, define, and analyze it, without being injured by it.

Take It and Get Lost

Unfortunately, such a spiritual position is not exactly popular among secular Jews in Israel today. As a result of cumulative fatigue, of shameful disputes, of religious coercion and religious politicking, many secular Jewish Israelis now tend to say impatiently: "All right! Enough! The hell with all of it—the Bible, the Talmud, the writings, the legends, the traditions, the prayers. Let the Orthodox fanatics take it and get out of our lives." For such secular Jews, the Bible has acquired, one might say, an aroma of black clothes, long beards, Yiddish, "settlements" in the West Bank, gunshots, and repression. This aroma is the source of the tendency to dump the whole heritage into the hands of the fanatics, muttering, "Take it and get lost!" and to make do with light comedy, rock music, and

200

imported cultural merchandise (some of it, admittedly, excellent).

Along with this extreme renunciation of Jewish heritage, we find its obverse: self-belittlement, in comparison with the Orthodox. Many secular Jewish Israelis consider such religious leaders as the Rebbe of Satmar, the Lubavitcher Rebbe, and the baba Baruch to be the *real* Jews, the "National League" of Jews, as it were. Next comes the "second team": the residents of Orthodox West Bank settlements and their fellow travelers. On the next rung down are "traditional" Jews: those who keep a kosher home, fast—at least on Yom Kippur—and drive on the Sabbath, but not to nonkosher restaurants. Near the bottom of the heap are the "ordinary" Jews; and the lowest of the low are the leftists, the Arab-loving peaceniks, who scream like banshees whenever they think an injustice has been committed.

Against this attitude, Lova Eliav flings out a challenge: The Bible is not the Satmar Rebbe, and the heritage of Israel is not the sole property of the West Bank settlers. The peace-lovers and those outraged by acts of injustice are, at least in their own eyes, not less, but more, "Jewish" than the defacers of "provocative" roadside advertising, murderers of Arab youths, and exhumers of dead converts to Judaism. Eliav's concept of Judaism calls for neither a sense of inferiority nor an apologetic posture, lowered eyes—perhaps for quite the contrary. His Judaism has no reason to feel embarrassed or unworthy, compared with the Orthodox.

At the same time, this does not mean that the Judaism of Zionists who hold progressive social views is above argument and beyond reproach. The Orthodox are within their rights to point out phenomena of spiritual decline or moral defilement among secular Jews, and to say, "Look where *your* concept of Judaism is leading you." Certainly a Judaism such as Eliav's must be prepared to defend itself, and, more important, to examine itself. It is more capable of doing so, in any event, than is the Judaism of the Orthodox, which never examines itself, except to ensure that it has remained a carbon copy of the kind of Judaism practiced by their fathers and forefathers.

True, revolutionary Zionist Judaism has had a number of extremely pretentious expectations, which were not realized. Far from it, in fact. But who can say that the effort to build a creative, just, self supporting society—even if that effort has managed to fulfill only ten or even five percent of its dreams— is any less Jewish than the strict separation of milk and meat dishes? Who can say that the struggle for peace is less sacred, or less Jewish, than the shaven or covered heads of married Orthodox women? Who can say that the attempt to establish a model of social justice, with neither exploitation nor oppression, is less Jewish than attaching a mezuzah to every doorpost?

Lova Eliav reads and studies the Bible from the standpoint of a legitimate heir. He does so in the manner practiced by teachers and interpreters of Judaism in former generations. He plays up some points and tones down others; he marks some verses with a thick blue line of admiration, and circles others with a strong warning red. The Bible, he says, contains not only the words "The wolf also shall dwell with the lamb" and "Nation shall not lift up sword against nation," but also such statements as "You shall save alive nothing that breathes." It contains universalist verses such as "Are you not as the children of the Ethiopians to Me, O children of Israel?" but also spiteful lines like "O daughter of Babylon, that art to be destroyed; happy shall he be, that repayeth thee as thou hast served us. Happy shall he be, that taketh and dasheth thy little ones against the rock." There is the idea of "Visiting the iniquity of the fathers upon the children unto the third and fourth generation," but also "Every man shall be put to death for his own sin." These contradictions have been explained, smoothed over, and reconciled by former generations of sages and commentators, but the Jews of the present generation are no less entitled to interpret the contradictions or to choose between them.

Take the concept of the Chosen People, for example. Among the interpretations are some really monstrous ones, supported by biblical references ("Moab is my washpot; unto Edom do I cast my shoe" and "And they shall fly down upon the shoulder of the Philistines in the west"). It is, however, both possible and preferable to interpret the concept of a Chosen People as a commitment, which assumes that the people have been "chosen" to fulfill obligations, without entitling them to any privileges whatsoever. It is both possible and preferable to undo the currently fashionable link between the concept of the Chosen People and the contemptible, abhorrent concept of a Master Race. This is a matter of interpretation; and those who leave the field of interpretation in primitive hands should not be surprised by the spreading of primitive interpretations.

Considered . . . as Cardinal

In the foreword to his book Lova Eliav says: "This book focuses on a study of seven ethical values expressed in the Bible, and considered by this author as cardinal: the sanctity of life, justice, freedom, equality, brotherhood, mercy, and peace." To my mind, this is an important sentence—not because of the mystical number seven, nor because of the well-wrought cataloguing of values, nor because of the, alas, somewhat deflated expression "ethical values." To me, the importance of this sentence lies in six words clustered at its center: "considered by this author as cardinal."

Eliav does not claim that these are, in fact, *the* cardinal values of the Bible. Nor does he claim that these values were considered by our forefathers as cardinal; nor even that they must be cardinal at all. No. In his words, they are "considered by this author as cardinal." This is a position involving both humility—anyone else is entitled to emphasize other values—and spiritual independence—Eliav asks no one's permission before deciding what he feels is worthy of being considered cardinal. In this matter, he accepts neither the authority of former generations nor the conventions of the religious establishment.

True, considerable support may also be found in the Bible for the opposite of those values: support for holding life in contempt, for intolerance, oppression of other people, discrimination, hatred, cruelty, and aggression. Eliav does not ignore it. He brings up well-known examples of such Biblical justifications for injustice and tribalism and analyzes their terrifying significance. But his basic premise is that every generation, and every reader, has the right to decide what is to be marked in approbatory blue, what is to be emphasized in warning red, and what is not to be stressed at all for the moment. To give but one example, the Bible certainly contains the story of the merciless wars of Joshua, son of Nun, which are currently quite fashionable as backing for a policy of cruelty and savagery against the Arabs; but it also tells how King Solomon presented twenty of the cities of the Land of Israel to King Hiram of Tyre. Yet Solomon was not struck down by divine fire and brimstone; nor is he condemned by any of the Prophets for donating part of his realm. Modern-day rightist Israeli factions would have treated pious King Solomon as a traitor and destroyer of Israel for making "territorial concessions." Imagine, though, what would happen if a present-day "king" of Israel suddenly decided to transfer twenty cities to a neighboring country; imagine what sort of epithets would be launched at him, not to mention sticks, stones, and, quite conceivably, bullets.

Eliav's insistence on the right to select the values "considered by this author . . ." is, in my opinion, a classic Zionist act; and no less the act of a free Jew. For, after all, the struggles in Israel are not being waged between the "keepers of the Bible" and those who renounce it, or between "good" Jews and "tainted, Europeanized" Jews. They are being waged between differing concepts of Judaism—some of them humanitarian, others tribal and primitive, and still others midway between. And all of them, unfortunately, are deeply rooted in the Bible and in other Jewish religious texts.

Lova Eliav wrote *New Heart, New Spirit* in an attempt to extricate the Bible from the hands of those who wield it like a club; in an attempt to emphasize the humanitarian light that shines forth from some portions of it. As he writes: *"New Heart, New Spirit*, then, represents an attempt to raise once again the banner of human values—Jewish and universal—sanctified in the Great Book, as well as an appeal to rally around that banner."

Lova Eliav, choosing to face the future, looks back toward the Bible in hope of having some effect on what will come to pass following these present evil times.

Davar, October 17, 1986

Eulogy for Ephraim Avneri

(Avneri died on Friday, May 21, 1982, about two weeks before the start of the war in Lebanon.)

It is difficult to part from you. All your life you disliked big words. If I try to express even a little about you, I will have to beware of your reprimand at our regular lunch table in the kibbutz dining hall, as you turn your penetrating blue eyes toward me and let your sharp wit fly, together with a juicy Jewish anecdote, as you always did.

But at the risk of infuriating you, I will say something now. All your life you were a handsome man, immaculate. You had in you the energy of dreams, the temperament of a world reformer; you were without a speck of zealotry or hatred. You were a realistic revolutionary, practical, keen, untouched by the dust of pettiness, a man with clear, strong beliefs and opinions, but without a shadow of dogmatism. You were saturated to your fingertips in Jewish melodies, yet even in your old age your eyes were turned more toward the future than back to the past. You were devoted to ideology, but capable of forgiveness, compromise, and humor.

You told me much about your childhood, about the Galician town where you were born, your rebellious youth, and the secret agonies you suffered because of your rebellion, suffering that lasted all your life. I carry your story like a precious pledge.

Your whole life was a struggle. You often struggled with your comrades here at Kibbutz Hulda, sometimes even with the teachers and mentors you so admired, and you struggled unceasingly with yourself. Doubt and hesitation accompanied you like a secret inner melody—in the youth movement in Galicia, in the village of Migdal when you first settled in this country, during the hard early years at Kibbutz Hulda, during your years of public service, and afterward when, at the age of fifty-some, you began to study as an undergraduate for a university degree, until the years of your illness, when you returned home to take upon yourself in your last years the job of a local telephone switchboard operator for the kibbutz exchange. You never ceased to be a man who lives by his faith but is fascinated by heresy. And because of this inner struggle you always radiated wisdom and charm.

In all the struggles that took place at Kibbutz Hulda during the last thirty years, at least, you always favored tolerance, consideration, and compromise with individual vagaries, even though some of those vagaries made your blood boil. And the more readily you forgave the weaknesses of others, the more severely you judged yourself. Perhaps that was why you were a brilliant, persevering student all your life, yet refused to become a teacher; a warm, close friend who refused to become a leader, even when you were called to leadership. You were an indefatigable man of action, yet you avoided power and position like the plague.

In a taped conversation with my daughter, Fania, about the early years at Hulda, you told her, "It would be worthwhile to talk someday about what it meant for a boy of twenty to arrive in this country alone, without a home, without a family, without a woman, as solitary as a cut-off finger . . . and the kibbutz is the only place where you had any emotional connections. It took me several years to understand that the kibbutz is not just a farm or a village, as some referred to it, but primarily the emotional connection, the extended family, the relationships. . . ." Everyone who knew and loved Ephraim Avneri can hear the sound of his voice in these words. Perhaps they comprise a kind of last will and testament: This is what we should try to be.

It is difficult to part from you. My peers frequently opposed you and your generation, the founders of Kibbutz Hulda. We argued, rebelled, ridiculed. Now, as we part from you, as we, too, have passed the halfway mark, we ought, quite simply, to tell you and your comrades, your generation: You are special. In thousands of years, the Jews have not produced a group of people who could compare with you. Who knows how many generations will pass before another group of dreamers and doers like you comes forth?

We have lost a beloved father, one of the founders of this place, one of the fathers of this wonderful, awesome era. For me, too, Ephraim was as precious as a father. Precious man, may our love go with you and may your spirit be with us.

Of Dreams and Dreamers

(Remarks made on the occasion of receiving the Bernstein Prize for Literature, September 1983)

This weekend is the tenth anniversary of the Yom Kippur War, after which it became a little more difficult to say, "The Arabs are no problem" or "Time is on our side." Sixteen years have passed since the victory of the Six-Day War, that just and tragic victory which began a new era, the victory followed by the fall of the State of Israel and its replacement by "The Land of Israel." It is a year and a half since the beginning of the "lightning strike" in Lebanon that was supposed to be a matter of a few days and has become a filthy war, wreaking havoc on us and on others. None of us will ever again be what he was before these wars.

Forgive me if I stand here and count wars. This is supposed to be a literary event. And some of us expect literature to provide us with comfort and consolation, or at least a few moments of mercy and grace, or at the very least a little distance and perspective. But I have neither comfort nor consolation, and I have no distance. I tell you that what was is no more. The truth is that for several years I have felt like an exile in my own land. (Not exiled from my land—that is a different

209

condition, in which you are, as the medieval poet Judah Halevi put it, "in the West while your heart is in the East." No. I mean exiled inside your own country. You are here and your heart is here, yet you are in exile. It is as though you woke one morning to find that someone had switched the city around, reversed the boulevards, shrunk or enlarged the streets, moved the squares from here to there—not just their names, but the streets and squares themselves. Everything is utterly familiar and yet utterly different, strange and scary, as in a nightmare.)

Very well. I know it is not polite to talk about politics when you are awarded a literary prize. So let us talk of literature. Before Zionism became tangible in the form of buildings and fields, factories and tanks, it was found in books. It is an undertaking that began almost entirely in books. People in torment, with dreams and nightmares, sat and painted with words a certain scenario—in all sorts of variations—a certain proposal to rescue themselves from their Jewish troubles. Or from the troubles of the Jews. Or from both. After reading these books, certain people, some of them apparently very strong people, sought to turn what they'd read into reality. All of the dreams. No less. "There in the lovely land of our fathers all our hopes will come to pass." All of them. Not just one or two hopes. And there were those who dedicated their entire lives to the task of making the various dreams travel from the books into reality. They thought that transforming a dream from a book into a living reality was like extracting a pearl from an oyster. They didn't know that it is, instead, like taking a tropical fish out of tropical waters. And so, along the way, something went wrong. Something snapped. Sorrow and war came. Dark impulses and lusts emerged, pretensions and all kinds of madness. Something didn't work out according to plan.

The Zionist dream was wonderful and awesome. It had elements of madness and despair side by side with elements of lucidity and even ironclad logic. The dreamers sought the impossible, yet they did, in wisdom, in cunning, and with an acute sense of reality, what was possible. Despite everything, Zionism is the best and straightest idea to have sprung from the twisted Jewish mind in two thousand years. That is my opinion, despite everything we have done and everything that has happened to us here. But something snapped along the way. Everyone knows it, including those who don't want to know.

Some of it can be repaired. Not all. I don't know how to fix it. I have tried, in what I have written, to bear witness, to record, to the best of my ability, cautiously and precisely, what there is here, what they hoped would be, what the dreams were and who the dreamers were; to record what happened.

If I were to speak, here and now, of everything on my mind, I would spoil the party. If I did not speak, I would be ashamed that I had not spoken. Words, I know, often falsify. But silence is often just a shameful use of speech.

The State of Israel
versus the Land of Israel

(Based on remarks delivered at a symposium at the Tsavta Club in Tel Aviv following the publication of Amos Kenan's book *To Your Country, To Your Homeland*. Participants: writer Yitzhak Ben-Ner, writer Amos Kenan, general Avraham Yaffe, and Amos Oz. Poet Naomi Shemer was invited, but was unable to attend.)

. . . First of all, I would like to take issue with Avraham Yaffe's statement here that "the Land of Israel is a living creature." That is not true. It is we who are living creatures. The land is not. The land is our place, a place without which we would surely be different people. This makes it an important place for us, but not a living creature. . . . Unlike Kenan, Yaffe, and Naomi Shemer, I am not one of those who "love the Land of Israel—as distinct from the State of Israel." I positively love the State of Israel just a little. At least sometimes I do.

Kenan asks whether there is really such an entity as the State of Israel. Answer: Yes, there is. I am ready to draw its borders on the map, and I will do so gladly. Kenan writes about the hills of the Land of Israel, "boulders at the top, cyclamen, hyssop. It was there." And he adds, "For fear of the evil eye, I do not want to say where"—lest, heaven forfend, we come there en masse, with picnic baskets, and despoil the Land of Israel for him. Kenan writes further about "the quick, sharp, cruel transition from the State of Israel to the Land of Israel, the land of the Bible. . . . You pass through this endless

Tel Aviv suburbia, not knowing whether you have left Tel Aviv and entered Herzliya . . . or is it all Kfar Saba? You pass tens of thousands of stereo systems, tens of thousands of acres of wall-to-wall carpeting . . . hundreds of thousands of acres of wallpaper . . . a sea of Formica countertops and forests of television antennas. That is what the Sharon plain once was and this is what it is now. And then—bang, all at once you are in the Homeland."

Note: He crossed the Green Line into the West Bank— and arrived in the Homeland. "Bang," as he puts it.

Furthermore: "The rocky slopes are no match for them who took the groves of the Sharon plain and turned them into full-color stereo. . . . They have no chance against them. Here are the Formica and wallpaper fields of the future: Karne Shomron, Har Kabir, Kaddum [West Bank Jewish settlements]."

I laughed out loud when I read this. Not at the misfortune of Kaddum and Karne Shomron, but at the meeting point that comes to light here between Kenan, the leftist dove, and Shemer, the passionate annexecutionist of the West Bank. A completely incredible marriage, it would seem, between Mr. Kenan, a former member of a right-wing prestate underground who now supports the partition of the country and the establishment of a Palestinian state, and Ms. Shemer, a daughter of Kibbutz Kinneret who now strives to keep every inch of the land. Both of them, it turns out, love the Land of Israel very much, and both of them do not love the State of Israel very much at all. Kenan crosses the Green Line and, bang, he is in the Homeland, which is also the sentimental homeland of Shemer: picturesque village, groves, cisterns, and other charms of the biblical Orient masquerading, for some reason, as the domain of the Palestinians. So I view this "match" between Kenan, Shemer, and Yaffe with something verging on amusement. It is always fascinating to see how people set out on a journey through space when, in fact, they want to journey through time—or the opposite: They travel through time when they really ache for other places. A person who wants to return to biblical times or to some sort of prebiblical Orientalism ups and crosses the Green Line and bang. A person who wants to return to the days of his youth ups and goes to a "pioneering outpost" in Sinai. Someone else, nostalgic for his parents' home in the Jewish shtetl of Eastern Europe, ups and tries to re-create the Kingdom of David and Solomon from the year 1000 B.C.E. Not to mention someone who longs to live in America and creates around him, by mistake, something not unlike the Jewish Warsaw of fifty years ago, convinced that it is an America.

I observe these phenomena from within the State of Israel. To be more precise, from Kibbutz Hulda, located in the coastal plain.

I am in favor of dividing the Land of Israel between its two peoples, and so is Kenan. But my motive is not to save the biblical character of Judea and Samaria from the perils of Formica and wallpaper. I admit it: I think there are things more beautiful than barren, rocky slopes, although I would be happy if at least some of them remained.

The title of this evening's symposium, "How to Return to the Land of Israel," is not entirely clear to me. We *are* in the Land of Israel. This basement, here in a high-rise building in Tel Aviv, is also the Land of Israel. The Formica fields are also the Land of Israel. Just as "Savings and Loan Village," Building 3, or Housing-Plan 8, or Workers' Co-op City 13 are the Land of Israel. Unless the hidden intention tonight is to present the Land of Israel in contradistinction to the State of Israel in order to negate the State of Israel. And maybe this is the covert common denominator that unites Mr. Kenan, General Yaffe, and Ms. Shemer. Now if they were negating it in the name of some visionary paragon, it would be understandable. But they are negating it in the name of sentimental exoticism.

If, in many respects, Israel is becoming more and more like the Jewish diaspora, I think that no Jewish settlement in the West Bank will restore its "youth" or its "Israeliness." Certainly the areas whose character is Palestinian will not give it a biblical dimension. As long as the diaspora dictates their priorities and tastes, Israelis will take the diaspora with them wherever they go. In order to free ourselves from it, there is no point in turning our gaze to "unsullied," "uncorrupted" geographic regions, because the issue is not one of space. In this respect, Kenan is right and his words are true and important: one builds his home and his garden according to his personality. I would say according to his mentality, but only Arabs have a "mentality." Or else a person builds his home and his garden according to the shape of his dreams and his yearnings. If he is dreaming of America, then he will build America everywhere he goes, in every landscape. Actually, he will not build America, but a fantasy of what his imagination perceives America to be, unrelated to the real America. He will furnish his room in this manner, no matter whether it is on a mountain in Samaria or on a mountain overlooking the Jezreel Valley. The rocky mountain will take on the likeness of its inhabitants despite the archeological digs, the biblical memories, and the remnants of antiquity.

There is also a reverse process: The individual is shaped by his environment; man is shaped by climate, flora, and landscape. But this process, unlike the other, is measured in hundreds of years, not in terms of a generation or two.

Archeological digs have little to say to me, even though roots in the past are important to me. Which past? Which roots? My mother and father, my grandparents—what happened before their time fascinates me in books, not in physical artifacts. For me, the Land of Israel of the distant past is in books, not in shards. After reading the words of the prophets, the adventures of the kings, the Song of Songs, what can shards add? It is as though, after I had read Dostoevsky, someone were to bring me a matchbox from St. Petersburg. By the way, the shard and the matchbox can, of course, help to illustrate continuity or to arouse the imagination, but they do not have the power, by themselves, to arouse emotions—in me. In these times, I should also add the following: We must fight for the right of archeologists to conduct their digging, in the face of ultra-Orthodox opposition, unrelated to the subjective experiential weight of pottery shards. The words of the prophets are infinitely more important to me than the discovery of a prophet's bones, or the unearthing of the stones our forefathers used to throw at the prophets. The hills of Samaria and Judea are places I would describe as "pretty," "interesting," "appealing," if only they were not the arena of a terrible tragedy for two peoples today, if they were not filled today with hatred, injustice, and danger for everyone, inhabitants and occupiers alike. It is hard for me to describe such an arena of tragedy as "picturesque," "esthetic," or "touching."

I can't help it, I don't always like the State of Israel, but sometimes I love it. In another, nontragic situation, I could perhaps find all kinds of picturesque biblical Arab villages on the West Bank esthetically appealing, but they are not me. And I am not enamored of them, not in the fashion of Ms. Shemer and not in the manner of General Yaffe or Mr. Kenan.

I would like the Jews here to change. That—yes. To become reconciled with themselves, with a history full of disaster, madness, and neurosis. To become a little reconciled with one another. Perhaps then, in the course of time, they will make peace with the place. Then, but only then, will the building, the house, the garden, the neighborhood, and the city be more content—in other words, more beautiful. As long as we don't attempt to "reconstruct our lost childhood." Neither our individual childhoods, of British Palestine, with ponytails and bobby sox and the pastoral fields of Jezreel, nor our collective childhood, with flocks of biblical sheep grazing on the slopes of biblical mountains. Because any such attempt is neurotic. And because no such attempt can succeed: What was once will not come again. Even if we want it awfully, terribly much. Even if we long for it endlessly. Hebron and Nablus will not be ours, whether or not the prophets once walked there, whether or not the stones our ancestors liked to throw at the prophets still lie scattered there. They will not be ours, and when they are not, it will be better for everyone.

We have to concentrate on the State of Israel, to want it and to put our efforts into it, to work on it and to struggle over its soul and shape. Perhaps it really will become slightly Mediterranean, more content, more relaxed, and a little more beautiful.

With that goal in mind, there is no point in going to war against the Formica and the wallpaper. To that end we have to change something inside ourselves. The change cannot be revolutionary, a change through a "bang." It will be, if at all, a gradual and very slow change, since it will be, it seems, a very profound one.

There is no point in feuding with the State of Israel, crossing the Green Line to breathe the aroma of the Palestinian/biblical orchards and olive groves, of the mint and the hyssop, and then shut our eyes and declare, "I've reached the Homeland." And there is certainly no point in saying, as Kenan does, "The State killed the Homeland for me." For better or for worse, or even for worst, the State is the Homeland. Especially when, at last, after Kenan and I overcome Shemer and Yaffe and return the occupied territories to the Palestinians. Afterward, perhaps, we will try to change ourselves—if that is still possible.

Different version in *Proza*,
February 1982

Make Peace, Not Love

The peace on the agenda now is peace between Israel and Palestine led by the PLO (or perhaps by the PLO under a different name). Peace between Israel and Jordan, between Israel and "a Palestinian autonomy," or between Israel and the West Bank Village League—is no longer relevant. It does not matter why it is no longer relevant, or whether or not this is a good thing, or whether or not such peace was ever relevant—presently the question of peace is between Israel and Palestine.

The Labor Party, under the leadership of Yitzhak Rabin, is incapable of endorsing peace between Israel and Palestine. As long as it is dominated by the ghosts of Golda Meir, Moshe Dayan, and Yisrael Galili, it is hard to see Labor freeing itself from policies that are no longer viable.

The non-Zionist Left is equally enslaved by dogmatism: not only does it accept most of the PLO's positions, in large part it endorses the PLO and identifies with it. As a result, it has no chance to influence.

So it is the Zionist Left that must be involved in achieving peace between us and Palestine—on the condition that Israel's security is guaranteed. We must make peace, but we must not start hugging the PLO with songs of praise.

Rivers of pain, grief, and anger are dividing Israelis and Palestinians. Let us not forget that for sixty years the Palestinian national movement maintained a policy of genocide against the Israeli Jews ("Idbach al Yahud!"—"Butcher the Jew!"). Until very recently it officially called for the destruction of Israel as a nation-state. Now it has abandoned (only verbally, perhaps) its demand for Israel's destruction. We should not underestimate the importance of verbal changes (indeed, every historical change of heart is always heralded by a verbal change). Yet the dovish Left must retain its perspective. The issue is making peace with a deadly enemy, not because deep down under his wolf's clothing he is actually a lamb, but precisely because he is a deadly enemy who now says he is ready to talk peace. We must pursue the possibilities with caution and sobriety, not with an outburst of sentimentality.

The issue is the partition of the land between its two peoples, a position which political Zionism had endorsed on numerous occasions in the past. Only with the rise of the Begin government to power in 1977 did Israel withdraw this proposal. We must reassert it in principle, while formulating our terms for such a partition: no foreign army must ever enter the territories from which Israel withdraws. If it does, this ought to be regarded as a violation of the peace treaty. The government in those territories should be held accountable for any form of attack or harassment into Israel. There must be a strong commitment to refrain from entering into military alliances with other powers. Any breach of such a commitment will be regarded as a just cause for military action by Israel. The Israeli Left ought to be the first to demand action if peace is violated by the Palestinians once they have their own homeland.

There is no room for moral agonizing about Israel's claims for border restrictions in areas thinly populated by Arabs, since it is almost certain that one day Palestine and Trans-Jordan will be a single nation whose territory will be five or six times greater than the territory of Israel. If, in the meantime, Palestine feels crowded, let it present some territorial demands to the Kingdom of Jordan, where two-thirds of the population is Palestinian anyway, and where there is plenty of empty land.

Immediately after peace is made between Israel and Palestine, Israel must grant and guarantee full equality for Israeli Arab citizens: equal rights, equal obligations, which includes military service and reserve duty with the IDF. Israeli Arabs will have to choose, freely and unambiguously, if they want to be Israelis in Israel, Palestinians in Palestine, or Palestinian citizens residing in Israel.

In the framework of a peace treaty, it would be possible to offer a parallel, symmetrical choice to the Jewish settlers in the West Bank and Gaza. They, in turn, will have to choose between becoming Palestinian citizens, or going to Israel, or remaining where they are as Israelis residing in Palestine.

The "target audience" of the Zionist Left, the public whose reason and emotion we must affect, are not the moderate Palestinians. First and foremost, we ought to address ourselves to those Israelis who distrust the Arabs and fear that peace is a trap. We ought to converse with these Israelis without condescension or deprecation.

Let us, then, put less energy into all those asymmetrical meetings between members of the Zionist Left and their Palestinian partners in dialogue, meetings which always result in joint condemnations of the Israeli occupation, and let us, instead, focus our energies on talking with the Israelis who are suspicious of the PLO and who fear the establishment of a Palestinian state under any conditions. Such a dialogue will

221

be fruitful only if the Zionist Left takes these suspicions and fears seriously. We must present a responsible and persuasive answer to the legitimate "hawkish" fear that "After Nablus and Gaza, those Arabs will want Jaffa and Haifa."

A recent poll indicates that fifty-four percent of the Jewish population in Israel is willing, under the right conditions, to negotiate even with the PLO. This means that tens of thousands of Likud voters and hundreds of thousands of Labor voters are ready to talk to the PLO. So, many voters supported the Likud not in order to prevent an Israel-PLO dialogue but because they assumed that it was preferable to have the Likud, rather than the Left, do business with Arafat. Perhaps because they fear that the Left might "sell its grandmother to the Arabs."

In the Palestinian world there is no counterpart to the Israeli intelligentsia, which is willing to enter into sharp confrontation with the Establishment and its prevailing ideologies. My intention here is not to assign low marks to the Palestinian people or to its intelligentsia but to emphasize that the Israeli intelligentsia must work to bring the statesmen to the bargaining table rather than attempt to negotiate in place of the statesmen: there is no point in negotiation between Israeli intellectuals and official or unofficial representatives of the PLO. This is not Vietnam, and there is no point in trying to imitate the gesture Jane Fonda made then (and now regrets). This is a war between Israel and the Arab world (which includes the Palestinians)—not a war between the Arabs and the Israeli Writers Association. It is not the Writers Association which must make peace with Palestine. The job of the intelligentsia is to persuade the majority of the nation that the policy makers ought to sit down and talk business with Mr. Arafat.

Israel has no legitimate and recognized leadership other than that of Yitzhak Shamir's government. One may find this regrettable, but there is no point in deluding the Palestinians that they can avoid the necessity of direct discussions with that government. Nor is there any value in "literary" peace treaties between oppositionist Israeli artists and Palestinian artists who are, almost always, a part of the PLO establishment.

In short, the Israeli intelligentsia must conduct neither a monologue with itself nor a dialogue with Palestinians. It must press, first and foremost, for an opening in the wall of resistance of those Israelis who are suspicious and fearful of peace.

It is both false and foolish to represent the Israeli-Palestinian tragedy as a civil rights campaign. The Palestinians are not our dark-skinned citizens suffering from discrimination. They are a neighboring nation, a defeated and conquered enemy. Arafat is not Martin Luther King. The academic freedom of Bir Zeit University is not the source of the tragedy nor the focus of it. Israel entered Nablus and Gaza in 1967 because of a real and immediate threat to its existence. We did not enter Nablus and Gaza in order to suspend people's civil rights or in order to shower them with civil rights. Once there is peace, we will pull out regardless of the status of civil rights there. The Palestinians in the West Bank and Gaza had very few rights before we entered, and we can assume, regretfully, that they. will not have much freedom, either, after we are gone.

The name of the game is not equalizing or integrating Palestinians and Israelis. The name of the game is a two-state solution. We owe the Palestinians one and only one right: the right to self-determination. Until that materializes, we must, of course, be alert and respond to any unconscionable acts that may be committed by the Israeli military government or by Jewish settlers on the West Bank and Gaza.

Claiming that the Palestinians are entitled to self-determination once Israel's peace and security are guaranteed, the

Zionist Left doesn't need to depict them as the "good guys" of the conflict, or to elevate them to the status of pure and innocent victims. There is certainly no reason to echo and defend every bit of nonsense or malevolence uttered by Palestinian leaders. Self-determination is not a prize awarded for good behavior. (If only good and righteous peoples, with a "clean record," deserved self-determination, we would have to suspend, starting at midnight tonight, the sovereignty of three-quarters of the nations of the world, beginning with both Germanys and Austria.) The Israeli Zionist Left errs when it tries to persuade the rest of the nation that the Palestinians are the underdog, that they're not really all that bad, that they don't really mean what they say and do, that deep down in their hearts they're nice and sweet and peace-loving.

We must not grant a "moral certificate" to the Palestinian national movement. By the same token, the deep soul-searching about the moral nature of our nationalism is not the business of the Palestinians, and we do not ask Arafat to convince his people that Israel is just and deserving of sovereignty. The matter is not one of gradations of morality, but of the decision of two enemies to choose life.

In order to persuade peace-fearing Israelis—but, even more, for the sake of its own integrity—the dovish Left must make a moral, ideological, and emotional commitment: to take up arms, to be the first to take up arms, if, after the establishment of a Palestinian state, the Palestinians try to implement what they call the "phase-by-phase strategy" by means of terror, military provocations against Israel, or the incitement of Israeli Arabs.

Spokespeople for the Zionist Left must be the first to condemn any Palestinian statement, issued in Arabic "for internal consumption," that calls for the destruction of Israel, such as that uttered by Arafat's second-in-command, Abu Iyad, less than a week after America's recognition of the PLO. According to Abu Iyad's statement, broadcast in Kuwait, an Arab state in Palestine is only the first step on the road to a completely Arab Palestine.

The Left should not leave condemnation of such statements to the Right. It should not squirm in an attempt to explain that Abu Iyad didn't really mean it, was misunderstood, had a deprived childhood, doesn't really represent anyone, or has no real command of Arabic. . . .

Inasmuch as the Labor Party, under the leadership of Yitzhak Rabin, does not appear to be committed to making peace, the Zionist Left will have to reach out to the hearts of hundreds or thousands of Labor voters and tens of thousands of Likud voters and try to convince them that there is no substitute for an Israeli-Palestinian agreement, and that the time has come to examine what is true and what is false in the PLO's new policy. This can be done by means of direct negotiation between Israel and the PLO. To open such negotiations, we ought to change minds in Israel itself. This cannot be done by insulting the hawks, scandalizing or infuriating them.

We would do well to separate the struggle for Israeli-Palestinian peace from other important issues. It is not wise to offer peace to the Israeli public as one part of a package deal that includes public transportation on the Sabbath, the abolishment of censorship, or the rights of nude sunbathers. There is no reason to tie the issue of peace to matters that many Israelis consider unacceptable for religious, moral, or bourgeois reasons. The correlation of peace with issues of "permissiveness" furthers neither the cause of peace nor of individual rights.

Achieving peace takes priority over the other battles that the intelligentsia is fighting. It may also affect the outcome of those other battles.

The arena is not Bir Zeit University in the West Bank. It is the neighborhoods of Jerusalem and Tel Aviv. More precisely, it may be not the central square of Tel Aviv but the development towns.

The battle is not a "defense" of the Palestinians or support of their cause. Rather, we should emphasize the necessity, the logic of the partition of the land between its two peoples, and the advantages and benefits it will bring. We must recognize that Israeli gut anger at Palestinian "behavior" is at least as understandable, human, and legitimate as Palestinian anger at us. In short, we are talking about peacemaking, not a honeymoon: *Make Peace, Not Love.* . . .

In light of recent polls, perhaps the time has arrived for the leadership of the struggle for peace to pass from the hands of the intellectuals—writers, artists, professors, and journalists—to other people. As long as the dovish intelligentsia was a voice crying in the wilderness, it played a courageous and pioneering role in the struggle for mutual recognition and peace between the two peoples. But since the basic recognition of the existence of two peoples and the need to talk with the PLO is now accepted by a majority of the Jews, the intelligentsia would do well to turn the cockpit of the peace movement over to other components of Israeli society—and the sooner the better. Continued identification of the cause of peace with writers, artists, and professors, as though it were their private concern, may be disastrous to peace as well as to that selfsame intelligentsia.

Although the Right will probably reject the following proposal, the Left ought to offer it as a basis for a national dialogue: Let the Right soften its position regarding talks with the PLO and compromise between the two peoples, and the Left will solemnly pledge itself to defend the borders of peace and see to the implementation of every last clause and comma in the peace treaty. In spite of the labels attached to us, we are not a "pacifist" Left nor are we doves who "turn the other cheek." We are Israeli patriots who believe that peace is not only necessary but also possible. And when the day comes that our swords are beaten into plowshares, we will make sure that it is not only Israeli swords that are so recycled.

—*Yediot Aharonot*, December 30, 1988

The Heart of the Fear

When a demilitarized Palestine is established alongside Israel and is at peace with us, it will be a country whose area is one-fifth the size of Albania and whose population is smaller than that of Kuwait. Every part of its territory will be within firing range of conventional Israeli weapons.

How then can we explain the murky, primeval fear that the idea of creating such a Palestinian state inspires in the hearts of even rational Israelis? How explain the amazing fact that Israel would rather fight another ferocious war, and another, and yet another, against all of the Arab states—including Iraq with its fifty battle-hardened divisions, Syria with its hundreds of new fighter planes and thousands of tanks, and Saudi Arabia with its monumental arms stockpiles and endless resources—than make peace with a tiny Palestine? Israel behaves as though it is ready to withstand a protracted conflict against the entire Moslem world, against the entire Third World, against the Communist Bloc, the European Common Market, and perhaps even, one day, the United States—as long as it does not have to coexist with a tiny Palestine. Sometimes it seems that Israel is willing to suffer a deep internal rift that may destroy the willingness of half its citizenry to fight, rather than tolerate a two-state solution; to do anything to avoid living next to a fifth of Albania or half of Kuwait—and even that, only on condition that Palestine be demilitarized and free of foreign armies.

How can we understand this lunatic phenomenon: Israel prepared to take on the whole world in order to prevent the danger of peace with a neighbor whose actual dimensions are going to be municipal, almost? Mr. Israeli, so it seems, is brave enough to challenge the whole world—and cowardly enough to fear a coexistence with a "pocket Palestine." Heard on a bus: "This George Bush is a big hero inside his White House. Let's see what he's like when he tangles with us." And, on another occasion: "If Arafat gets Kalkilya, he'll be in Tel Aviv within ten minutes."

Primeval, dark panic.

The courageous-cowardly Israeli will invariably respond with this stock answer: "If you give them Nablus and Gaza, tomorrow they'll want Jaffa and Haifa as well."

And if you don't give them Nablus and Gaza, they won't want Jaffa and Haifa?

And if they do want Jaffa and Haifa, what of it?

What, then, is the heart of the fear? What is the latent menace for us in a tiny Palestine? Why has the idea of a Long Island–size state between Hebron and Nablus turned into the straw that breaks the camel's back, into the pea that disturbs the sleep of the Israeli princess who has lain, for tens of years, on the explosive stack of mattresses of several large enemy nations?

Perhaps because Palestine arouses in us a dim, repressed sense of guilt: If retaining Nablus is a crime, then maybe retaining Jaffa and Haifa is also a crime. If this is indeed the

229

crux of the fear, the source of the mysterious sense of terror, then we need emergency shock treatment to bring us to the elementary understanding that the issue is not one of crime and punishment, the issue is the choice between life and death. We are talking not about guilt and penitence but about concluding a sensible deal between two parties with no love lost between them. Retaining Jaffa and Haifa was not—is not—a crime, for an abundance of reasons, but the simplest reason is sufficient: Without Jaffa and Haifa we cannot survive. Nablus and Hebron are an entirely different matter, for a number of reasons, the simplest among them being that we can live very well even if we discard them. Only the blind cannot see that we can barely survive if we do *not* discard them. The time has long since arrived for us to part from them peaceably, under conditions which will prevent them from threatening us in the future.

And if the Palestinians deceive us? It will always be easier for the Israel Defense Forces to break the backbone of the tiny Palestinian state than to break the backbone of an eight-year-old Palestinian stone thrower.

Davar, December 23, 1988

He Raises the Weak
from the Dust and Lifts
the Poor Out of the Dirt

I SAMUEL 2:8, PSALMS 113:7

(Remarks made upon receiving an honorary doctorate from the Hebrew Union College–Jewish Institute of Religion, Jerusalem, March 10, 1988)

Mr. President, honored guests, and friends:

With your permission, I would like to speak today not about exceptions to the norm but about the norm itself; more precisely, about new standards that have become increasingly common. It is not difficult to denounce a gross deviation, to bring a monstrous deviant to justice. One can punish the deviant as long as the standard itself is humane.

A short story from the tales of Israel: Long before the current Palestinian uprising, in October 1982, a man named Nissan Ishgoyev was driving the garbage truck that belonged to the Jewish settlement of Hinanit. Several children, among them a thirteen-year-old boy named Hisham Lofti Maslem, threw stones at the garbage truck driven by the man from Hinanit. The driver made a U-turn and went back. But before doing so, he got out of his truck for a moment, aimed his Uzi just a bit (not in warning, not to shoot at legs, but to wound and kill), fired—just a bit—straight from the hip, and killed thirteen-year-old Hisham—just a bit. Then he finished making his turn and continued on his way.

231

So far, it would seem, a deviation par excellence. And now for the norm. Five years have passed—which our man, Nissan, from Hinanit has not spent behind bars. In February 1988, the honorable Judge Uri Strosman passes sentence on the sharpshooter from Hinanit. First of all, he finds the accused guilty of manslaughter, a charge that, under the law, carries a sentence of up to twenty years in prison. But the judge sentences him only to six months' imprisonment, which, the judge declares, are to be completed not in jail but in community service. "There is no doubt," Judge Strosman writes in his decision, which I quote here verbatim, "that it is forbidden to shoot stone throwers. It would have been sufficient to fire into the air in order to disperse them." And another astonishing quote from this sensible judge: "In these turbulent times, children and young people should be under parental supervision." Turbulent times indeed! Parents who do not supervise their children carefully had better not be upset if their children get killed. And does a child who strays from the watchful eyes of his parents during these turbulent times deserve to die?

The question has already been raised: Would the man from Hinanit have shot to kill Jewish stone throwers in Jerusalem? Or a neighbor's child who had thrown a rock at his window or at his garbage truck? Would the honorable judge have settled for a sentence of six months of community service if the victim of the accused had not been an Arab child? If Hisham's bereaved parents, upon hearing Judge Strosman pronounce sentence, had burst into the courtroom, hurling epithets we are unfortunately accustomed to hearing on the playing field, wouldn't they have been punished more severely for contempt of court than was the killer from Hinanit?

It is all a matter of standards. You may ask why I mix dirty politics with a festive ceremony of awards at this distinguished academic institution. Very well. I do so because the issue here is not one of deviants or lunatic fringes. What is at issue here are basic values. And therefore I say that this is not a question of politics or security, not of borders and diplomacy. We are talking about the very essence of Judaism today, about the raison d'être of a Jewish state. And if the subject is, among other things, the essence of Judaism today and the purpose of a Jewish state, then it is not only permissible but also imperative that we deal with it, especially here and especially now.

The code of Hammurabi decrees one sentence, relatively light, for the killer of a slave who is old and tired. A harsher sentence is decreed for the killer of a slave who is young and in good health. The punishment for the killer of a free man is far more severe, and the most drastic penalty is reserved for one who has murdered an eminent figure, such as a judge. To our great consternation the leftists who legislated the Ten Commandments decreed only four simple, unambiguous words: "Thou shalt not murder." It was as simple as that, without classifications or categories. Perhaps they forgot to add, in parentheses, somewhere in between "Thou shalt not murder" and "Shall you murder and then inherit?" the phrase "Once an Arab, always an Arab." Perhaps they forgot to emphasize that the Ten Commandments apply only within the Green Line, and then only to a Jew born of a Jewish mother or converted according to Orthodox Halakah—except for leftists, who are worse than Gentiles.

Do I exaggerate? Do I overstate my fear of those who now sully not only the State of Israel, not only Zionism, but also Judaism itself? Several weeks ago, the Holy Spirit suddenly descended upon Israel's Chief Rabbi Eliyahu, whereupon he made a normative declaration of his own, in keeping with the spirit of ancient Israel and the best Jewish tradition: "We," said the venerable rabbi, "lifted the Arabs from the dirt and

233

they," he added sadly, "are not even grateful." This is indeed a weighty conundrum in Judaism. Who now "raises the weak from the dust and lifts the poor from the dirt"? And who is ungrateful? Well imagine, my esteemed professors, how the earth would shake if some anti-Semitic cardinal or archbishop in America should dare to say that "we Americans lifted those Jews from the dirt and they, alas, are not grateful." And in such a case, the sin of the archbishop would still be less than that of the venerable rabbi. The truth is that vast sums of American money have gone to improve the material situation of both Jews and Arabs in Israel, even though the enormous funds have actually reduced our ethics, perhaps, to garbage. But that is a different story.

And what is left of our Jewish heritage? Where have they dragged one of the world's most magnificent civilizations? What has this brand of Orthodox Judaism left us of Judaism? Much of Orthodoxy has reduced the Jewish heritage to one or two simplistic punches, such as angry, violent fanaticism about the sanctity of the Sabbath, or burning bus stations and throwing stones on the Sabbath, or the humiliating, public expulsion of converts whose conversion procedure was not exactly to their taste. Or preserving "the Greater Land of Israel" within the borders of 1967, even as they fan ferocious hatred of non-Jews in general and Arabs in particular; even as they fan hatred of Jews who believe that continued occupation of new territories will lead us to disaster. Who knows whether an Orthodox Jewish child raised in certain parts of Israel today is not raised and educated with the belief that the Ten Commandments include "Thou shalt not have mercy," "Thou shalt not concede," "Thou shalt not negotiate." There shall be no autonomy, no international peace conference, no compromise. Once an Arab, always an Arab. The only good Arab is a deported Arab. And to hell with the goyim. And—who

knows?—if someone were to come to Hillel the Elder in our
day and ask what is the essence of Torah, perhaps the answer
would be, as Professor Aviezar Ravitsky ironically said, that
the whole Torah can be found in the pleasant words "Thou
shalt oppress them and thou shalt transfer them."

I do not know. Some say that these are the birth pangs
of the peace process. Perhaps. It would be a sentimental mistake to expect that peace will begin with a procession of Arab
schoolchildren from Ramallah bringing flowers to the Jewish
children of Kibbutz Kiryat Anavim, or vice versa. Perhaps we
are witnessing the final convulsions of the Israeli-Palestinian
war, and of the Israel-Arab conflict. Perhaps. But if this is
indeed the case, we will have to commemorate this peace with
an enormous monument to blindness, stupidity, and folly.
Because in the end Israel will obtain what it could have ob-
tained, perhaps on better terms, ten years ago or maybe even
twenty-one years ago. And in the end the Palestinians will get
only a fraction of what they could have got peacefully and
honorably back in 1947, if it had not been for their fanaticism
and hostility. Only the dead will get nothing. Except wreaths.
Perhaps on the day that peace comes, the dead will have spit
into the faces of all of us, from Baghdad to Khartoum, from
Kibbutz Beit Alpha to the West Bank settlement of Karnei-
Shomron.

Very well. One must avoid simplistic symmetry like the
plague. To the question of who bears primary responsibility
for this tragedy, I reply, without hesitation: The primary historic responsibility is borne by the Palestinian national movement and its supporters in the Arab states and in the rest of
the world. The Palestinian national movement is, I believe,
one of the most stolid, wicked, and fanatical movements of
this century. It is sometimes difficult for me to understand
how so many decent people in the moderate Israeli camp are

235

capable of falling joyfully on the neck of a Palestinian Kahane or preparing a jubilant reception for a ship full of Palestinian Kahanists even while they justly denounce Jewish Kahanism. The goals and methods of the Palestinian movement have consistently been the same as the goals and aims of Meir Kahane: to destroy a nation and expel a people. If not worse. This is the national movement that has drenched us all, Jews and Arabs alike, in sixty-five years of blood and mire. We can only hope that we have not been infected by it now.

The question, however, is not merely who started it, who is to blame. And the issue is not "Look who's preaching morality to us." The question is not how we compare, morally, to many individuals and nations who preach morality to Israel. The primary, basic, overriding question is: How shall we live and not die? How can we save Israel from the threat of physical destruction and at the same time from the danger of moral and spiritual disintegration? How can we live and not die? If we can compromise, we will live, but if we behave like fanatics, we will die. All the rest is commentary. Go and learn.

No, I have not forgotten: We have met today for a ceremony in the realm of the intellect. This is not the place to talk politics. But I am not talking politics. The real argument that divides the nation today ceased long ago to be a dispute about territories, political parties, security, ancestral rights, and borders. This is an argument about the nature of Judaism and the image of man. The question is not whether these Palestinians are really a people or perhaps just a hodgepodge of laborers, hewers of wood and drawers of water by day and terrorists and murderers by night. The question is not: Who are the Palestinians? The question is: Who are we? Have we really deteriorated to the point where we can turn, with a self-righteous whine, to a hypocritical world and complain that

236

this same hypocritical world allows Assad to commit murder at his leisure, Brezhnev to oppress his neighbors, Qaddafi to rampage, and all this without a word to those bastards, but yells at us, rebukes us, doesn't allow us to get away with a little wantonness of our own, in peace and quiet; doesn't take into consideration the fact that we Jews are pitiful orphans, graduates of pogroms, concentration-camp survivors. Aren't unfortunates like us allowed to flex our muscles sometimes, too, like those big guys? In short: Tell me to whom you look for moral endorsement, and I will tell you who you are; who we are.

You see, again Hebrew literature stabs us in the back and gives aid and comfort to Israel's enemies. I'm sorry about that. It began with a leftist known as the Prophet Nathan, who insulted the name of King David and pictured him in all his ugliness, without considering that the shameful incident with Uriah the Hittite would be broadcast on all the TV stations, reaching every home in the world, giving anti-Semites cause for rejoicing. And this tradition was continued by that well-known defeatist Elijah, with the scandal over Naboth's vineyard. He was followed by all sorts of self-hating, publicity-seeking prophets. In their footsteps all sorts of mischief-makers have come in our time to trouble Israel: the poet Chaim Nachman Bialik, the novelists Mendele Mocher Seforim and Y. H. Brenner, and more recent writers. Their type has existed in every generation. And it is they who are the keepers of the flame, who have sustained the spirit of Judaism, not those who have stoned them in every generation.

Perhaps it is necessary, at this point, to ask from what source these contemporary writers and poets derive their authority? They have heard no voices from heaven; they are not prophets. Why, for the past one or two hundred years, have they stubbornly insisted on climbing on soapboxes and preaching to crowds? Who appointed them watchdogs of the House of Israel, to stand at the crossroads and presume to direct the traffic—or even stop it? What, if anything, do writers understand better than shoemakers do or glaziers or bakers or doctors—or even politicians? The fact is that there are two things about which writers may presume to have a certain degree of expertise. One is language. Contrary to the sentimental, romantic cliché, poets do not handle words as a lover handles bouquets. They treat words the way a bacteriologist treats germs. As a result of their work and their intimate, microscopic contact with language and its implications, they are sometimes able to detect disease or the threat of an epidemic before others do. Here is a small example, if you wish, not necessarily taken from the territories or from the realm of deviations and norms. For several years, we have been able to hear, in colloquial Hebrew, that the love life of the Israeli male is conducted somewhat like this: He meets a bombshell, puts her into a state of preparedness, and then lifts her off on a missile. Unless, that is, he gets torpedoed along the way.

When love uses language like this, it is a sign that the disease of violence has already filtered into the innermost tissues of our being. A sign that the war has stormed in and conquered even our beds. One who thinks and speaks of his beloved in such language . . . Better, perhaps, to leave this sentence unfinished. I want to emphasize that I am not talking about corruption of the language, but about blindness. Our language and, with it, our world are clouded by thick smoke.

The second thing that a writer or a poet may understand just a little better than many other people is what his fellow human being experiences. We writers, many of us, get up in the morning and, after a cup of coffee, begin to slip into the

other fellow's shoes. Or under someone else's skin. A fundamental rule of the profession is the necessity to ask oneself the
question: Suppose I were not I? Suppose I were he? or she?
or the neighbor? or someone else—my spouse, or the enemy?
In this respect the writer is not unlike a clever intelligence
agent. Perhaps due to their habit of getting into the shoes and
under the skin of others, many of the best poets and writers
see the Israeli-Palestinian war not as a cheap Western in which
the civilized good guys battle the savage, bloodthirsty natives,
but as a Greek tragedy: right against right—although, as I have
said, right against right does not mean, to me, an evenhanded
distribution of the burden of guilt. The blame rests mostly
with the Palestinian national movement. Nevertheless, even
the guiltier side may be a victim of the tragedy. There are
not—there have not been for some time—two separate tra-
gedies, Israeli and Palestinian, but only one, a tragedy that
envelops us all. Either we will be released from it together,
through painful but intelligent compromise, or else we will
perish in it together. We and they are bound together by
thousands of threads, shackled together like a prisoner and his
jailer. There already are elements of near intimacy in the
hostile relations between us and them, including similarities
that are peculiar, frightening, and sometimes almost ridiculous.

Let us return, for a moment, to the verse quoted by Chief
Rabbi Eliyahu: "He raises the weak from the dust and lifts the
poor from the dirt." For the venerable Rabbi Eliyahu, the
Israelis, incredibly, have become the Holy One, blessed by
He Who lifts the poor ungrateful Arab out of the dirt. But I
say to you that before there is peace, and particularly after
there is peace, we will have to lift our own humanity out of
the dirt. We will have to lift out of the dirt Judaism and

Zionism, both of which have come so close to falling captive to their distorters.

I ask your forgiveness for not speaking here today of sweetness and light.

NOTE: The state appealed, in the Israeli Supreme Court, the lenient sentence handed down by Judge Uri Strosman in the case of Nissan Ishgoyev. The Supreme Court accepted the state's arguments. On June 30, 1988, Nissan Ishgoyev was sentenced to three years in prison and two additional years on probation.

ACKNOWLEDGMENT

The Author wishes to thank David Twersky
for having helped in the selection
of the pieces for this volume.